Connecting with Baptism

Connecting with Baptism

A practical guide to Christian initiation today

Edited by Mark Earey, Trevor Lloyd and Ian Tarrant

 CHURCH HOUSE
PUBLISHING

Church House Publishing
Church House
Great Smith Street
London SW1P 3AZ

Tel: 020 7898 1451
Fax: 020 7898 1449

ISBN 978-0-7151-4110-6

Published 2007 by Church House Publishing

The opinions expressed in this book are
those of the authors and do not necessarily
reflect the official policy of the General
Synod of The Archbishops' Council of the
Church of England.

Typeset by RefineCatch Limited, Bungay, Suffolk
Printed in England by MPG Books Ltd, Bodmin, Cornwall

Contents

People

Policy

Preparation

Services

The contributors

The Group for the Renewal Of Worship (GROW) is the group of authors, liturgists, musicians and theological educators responsible for producing the Worship Series of booklets published by Grove Books. This book arises from our discussions about the way in which the *Common Worship* initiation resources focus the relationship between worship and mission, and the need for a guide or handbook to help people make the best use of the opportunities regularly presented to the Church by these services. Those who have contributed to the book include:

Patrick Angier, Vicar of St Peter's, Presbury, Cheshire

Colin Buchanan, Honorary Assistant Bishop in the Diocese of Bradford

Christopher Byworth, former Rector of St Helens, Lancashire

Mark Earey, Tutor in Liturgy and Worship at the Queen's Foundation, Birmingham

Anne Harrison, Co-ordinator of the Royal School of Church Music's Liturgy Planner, 'Sunday by Sunday'

Carolyn Headley, Priest-in-Charge of Warnford and West Meon, Hampshire and Co-ordinator of Education for Petersfield Deanery, Portsmouth

David Kennedy, Canon Precentor, Durham Cathedral, former member of the Liturgical Commission

John Leach, Parish Development Advisor for the Diocese of Monmouth

Trevor Lloyd, former Archdeacon of Barnstaple, former member of the Liturgical Commission

Peter Moger, National Worship Development Officer, Church of England

Gilly Myers, Succentor, Sacrist and Minor Canon of Durham Cathedral

Charles Read, Vice-Principal of the Norwich Ministry Course

Liz Simpson, Priest-in-Charge, West Buckingham Benefice

James Steven, Tutor in Worship and Doctrine, Trinity College, Bristol

Tim Stratford, Team Rector of Kirkby, Liverpool and member of the Liturgical Commission

Ian Tarrant, Senior Anglican Chaplain at the University of Nottingham

Phillip Tovey, Director of Reader Training, Diocese of Oxford and Lecturer in Liturgy, Ripon College, Cuddesdon

Preface

- Who comes to the Church asking for baptism these days?
- How can the Church respond positively to these requests?
- How does our practice of initiation connect with our mission and evangelism?
- What is the best way to prepare adults for Christian initiation?
- How can we follow up those who are baptized or confirmed and help them to grow in the faith?

These are just some of the many practical questions that churches face when looking at baptism, confirmation and the range of new services and opportunities provided in *Common Worship: Christian Initiation*. This book provides, in a down-to-earth and stimulating way, an enormous amount of practical help, background information and suggestions for clergy and lay leaders involved in taking policy decisions, providing pastoral care and using these services.

But behind these practical questions lurks a range of far-reaching issues about what exactly it means to be a Christian, how people become Christians, how the Church defines its boundaries and membership, and the very nature of the Church itself as it is being shaped by and for mission. The writers of this book are convinced that there is a connection between how we see these issues and how we deal with the practical questions. By focusing on baptism - the sacrament by which we are joined to Christ, joined to the Church, and commissioned for a lifetime of discipleship - the Church will find itself exploring the wider issues and being changed as a result.

All of the contributors to this book have a concern for the practice of baptism, and a desire to see it play its part in the mission of the Church. Many of us are parish clergy or chaplains who administer baptism regularly. Some of us have been involved in different ways with the creation and revision of *Common Worship: Christian Initiation*. What we all share is a belief that baptism matters. It matters to God, to the candidates and to the Church. It matters that we understand it and it matters that our practice of baptism is 'unpacked' in all its fullness, so that it can do what it is meant to do in the lives of individuals and communities.

We do not believe that any *particular* forms of service, on their own, are the answer to the Church's needs. We do, however, believe that the *Common Worship* services are useful tools that can allow the powerful message of God's love and God's call to reach not only our minds, but also shape our wills, our hearts, our churches . . . and our communities. This book sets out to help us use those tools as effectively as possible, and in the way that best fits each particular context. But running alongside that very practical purpose is a conviction that re-examining the meaning of baptism and living it out practically in the local church, using the tools provided by *Common Worship: Christian Initiation*, has the potential to renew the Church in a profound and lasting way.

Introduction: Finding the way

This is not a book designed to be read from cover to cover (though we hope that it will make sense if you choose to work through it in that way). It's meant to be a dipping-into kind of book, where people can begin to find some of the answers to questions about how starting out in the Christian life relates to the services and prayers in *Common Worship: Christian Initiation.* How can different points on the journey be marked? How can the services themselves be opportunities for welcome and growth in faith? And how does all that help the Church's task of mission? It is written for anyone looking for answers to questions like that, but particularly for clergy and lay ministers, for church leaders, members of church councils, and others involved in preparing adults, children, and whole families for baptism and confirmation.

Some sections will inevitably apply more to your situation than others. So, for instance, at various points there are questions for church councils (or other groups) to discuss. There are stories throughout the book and, again, some of these you will find you identify with, some not. There are four important stories fairly near the beginning of the book, in section A3, which show different routes by which people join the Church. Charts help to explain the routes, and there are links from these to different sections of the book to help you explore things further. Similar links occur throughout the book, to help you find what you want or follow up an interesting idea (e.g. ➤A7).

The book is arranged in five main sections, focusing on
- people, both church members and enquirers or candidates (section A);
- policy issues for ministers and church councils (section B);
- preparation of all involved (section C);
- the services themselves and what is involved in each (section D);
- pilgrims: what happens afterwards as people continue to grow in the faith (section E).

You may already have some particular questions that you want to explore, but if not, the range of real life stories on pages 12–18 may be a good place to begin your exploration of this book, and of the issues surrounding Christian initiation in the Church today.

References

For ease of reference, throughout the book you will find reference to the following, without the full details, which are given here:

CW Christian Initiation	*Common Worship: Christian Initiation*, Church House Publishing, 2006
CW main volume	*Common Worship: Services and Prayers for the Church of England*, Church House Publishing, 2000
CW Pastoral Services	*Common Worship: Pastoral Services*, Church House Publishing, 2000, 2005
Daily Prayer	*Common Worship: Daily Prayer*, Church House Publishing, 2005
New Patterns for Worship	*New Patterns for Worship*, Church House Publishing, 2002
On the Way	*On the Way: Towards an Integrated Approach to Christian Initiation*, Church House Publishing, 1995
Rites on the Way	*Rites on the Way: Work in progress, GS Misc 530*, Church House Publishing, 1998
Visual Liturgy	*Visual Liturgy Live*, the Church's electronic worship planner, Church House Publishing, 2007

Page references to *CW Christian Initiation* are preceded by the abbreviation *CWCI*.

The *Response by the House of Bishops to Some Questions Raised by Diocesan Chancellors* is available on the web site of the Diocese of Portsmouth (www. portsmouth.anglican.org), in Appendix 14 of the Diocesan Handbook (via the Resources link)

Unless otherwise indicated, biblical quotations are taken from the New Revised Standard Version.

Section

A

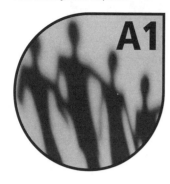

A1 PEOPLE

A Church shaped by baptism

'Start as you mean to go on!' - that, in a nutshell, is what this book, and baptism itself, is all about.

In this chapter we step back from the more detailed considerations about how baptism is prepared for, administered, and followed up, and look at the bigger picture of how baptism can shape the Church and its assumptions about itself, about God, and about how to live the Christian life.

Living out our baptism

The New Testament gives us no other way than baptism for individuals to express publicly their allegiance to Christ and their decision to follow him and to associate themselves with his people, the Church. The doorway into Christ and into the Church is baptism-shaped, and when we squeeze through it, we ought to be shaped by it. More than that, the Church itself, the body of those who have joined themselves to Christ, ought itself to be baptism-shaped too, not just in the sum of its individual parts, but in the shape of the 'whole' - the way it lives its life and structures itself. The Church is the community of the baptized.

'Churches are increasingly recognizing one another's baptism as the one baptism into Christ when Jesus Christ has been confessed as Lord by the candidate or, in the case of infant baptism when confession has been made by the church (parents, guardians, godparents and congregation) and affirmed later by personal faith and commitment. Mutual recognition of baptism is acknowledged as an important sign and means of expressing the baptismal unity given in Christ.'

Baptism, Eucharist, Ministry, World Council of Churches, 1982, page 6, para. 15

You only have to step back and look at the very basic things that baptism focuses to see the massive implications for individuals, their relationships one with another, and the corporate life of the Church:

Baptism says that Christians
● have been given a new identity in Christ;
● have made a decision to follow Christ on a lifelong journey;
● have turned away from sin and are living a new life;
● have received both forgiveness and the Holy Spirit;
● are brothers and sisters of Christ;
● share together in being 'in Christ';
● welcome newcomers to share their experience of God's love;
● will value and honour each other as reflecting Christ and sharing the Spirit.

These are not theoretical aspirations - they have practical implications every day.

All of this ought really to be obvious, given the important place that baptism has in beginning the life of faith, but it isn't always seen in this way. In recent years, in many parts of the Church, there has been a rediscovery of this central place that baptism has in shaping the life of the believer and the Church. The resulting 'baptismal ecclesiology' simply means taking seriously the way that baptism should not only mark the beginning of the Christian life, but also guide and shape the way that life develops, for the individual and for the Christian community. It means that we are a 'baptismal Church' – a Church shaped by baptism.

One of the signs of this recovery of the foundational nature of baptism is the primary place accorded to baptism in ecumenical discussions. There has been much agreement and understanding in areas such as the Eucharist, and ministry, but nowhere has that agreement been clearer than in relation to baptism as something that can unite churches and individuals. Once we can acknowledge one another as true believers in Christ, sharing in common our baptism into him (whatever the mechanics of the way that baptism is administered) then the other discussions become 'family disagreements' rather than alien encounters.

There are significant practical implications which follow from viewing baptism in this foundational way. Perhaps the most significant of these is the recognition of the Christian life as a journey. There is a journey through the baptism service itself, from presentation, through decision, profession of faith and baptism itself, to commission and prayer and being sent out to shine as a light in the world. But baptism is also a marker on the journey of life and faith. It will have been preceded by the work of God in drawing someone to Christ (and the responsibility of the Church to make space for new believers) and it will be followed by a lifetime of growing into all that it means to follow Christ.

Journey, story, pattern

In the spiritual formation of a new Christian there needs to be a healthy interaction between three aspects of the Christian life: journey, story and pattern.

Journey is a major image in the narrative of Scripture from the call of Abraham through to the itinerant ministry of Jesus and beyond. As an image of human life and of the passage to faith it allows both for the integration of faith and human experience and also for the necessity of change and development.

Liturgical representatives from the Anglican Communion met in Toronto in 1991 to consider the renewal of Christian initiation. The statement that resulted ('Walk in Newness of Life') called for a re-integration of mission and baptismal practice and was a significant part of the background to *CW Christian Initiation*.

'The journey into faith involves a process that includes awareness of God, recognition of God's work in Christ, entering into the Christian story through the scriptures, turning to Christ as Lord, incorporation into the body of Christ, nurture within the worshipping community, and being equipped and commissioned for ministry and mission within God's world. An adequate practice of baptism will recognize all these dimensions and will enable the church to play its full part in accompanying people in this journey.'

International Anglican Liturgical Consultation, Toronto 1991, quoted in the Introduction

CWCI, page 9

Closely related to journey is the importance in human and Christian experience of story. It is significant that the story of Paul's conversion is told three times in the book of Acts: Christian formation must allow an individual's story to be heard and to find its place within the unfolding story of faith as it appears in the Church and in the Scriptures.

Complementary to the ideas of journey or story is the theme of pattern or way. Essential to Christian formation is the appropriation of patterns of belief, prayer and behaviour that give structure and coherence to the Christian life. This is part of what the earliest Christians recognized when they called themselves The Way. The report *On The Way* gave careful attention to how patterns of life and faith are established in the life of the Christian and the Church. These services seek to recognize that journey and pattern are integral to the Christian life and need to be reflected in any approach to Christian initiation.

CWCI, page 9

Further implications

If baptism is to be allowed to do its work of shaping us for the journey of faith, there will be other practical implications:

The candidate

For the individual candidate, baptism needs to be treated as something which is significant and which marks the beginning of a new way of life. This may have an effect, for instance, on the way a local church handles enquiries from non-churchgoers about the

B2 ➤ baptism of their children. ◄

The practice of baptism

Baptism needs to be administered in a way that shows its significance, not only for the candidate concerned, but for the whole church. Each baptism service is a reminder of that baptism-shaped doorway through which we all have entered, and of the continual need to allow baptism, and all that it stands for, to shape us for living the Christian life. That might mean, for instance, changes to the way that baptism takes place, and an emphasis on baptism services as significant events for the whole church family, not just

B5, D10 ➤ the candidates and their families. ◄

The life of the local church

If preparing people for initiation is seen as accompanying them on a journey, and that preparation is conspicuous in the regular worship of the Church (as the Rites on the Way material in *Christian Initiation* suggests) then every worshipper is potentially shaped by those assumptions. At the heart of the Church's life will be a model of open relationships and a learning experience which is open to all and in which all have something to contribute. Like any journey, the particular experiences will depend on each individual, but travelling together means that different views are not seen as private and isolating, but discoveries to be shared and explored. This will have implications for a church's overall pattern of Christian learning, both on Sundays and during the week. ➤

➤**C1 - C6, E2, E3**

The church's sense of identity

When the church meets for worship, but perhaps most obviously when it gathers for the Eucharist, it meets as the community of the baptized. Baptism constitutes the community and defines its boundaries. Those who are in Christ share his peace, his bread and wine, and are his body: 'we are one body because we all share in one bread.' Others, who are not baptized, may be present as well, of course, but they are present as welcome guests of a core community – and guests who can choose to be incorporated themselves into this community. The admission of baptized children to communion ➤ highlights the relationship between baptism and ecclesiology, the theology of how the Church is. We are brought face to face with the fact that the Church is for everyone: young and old, people of every race, those with learning disabilities and those who find it hard to articulate the reasons for their faith. At Easter, and on other occasions, the Church renews its baptism vows, ➤ defines itself again and experiences then – and hopefully on other frequent occasions – the reality of new people finding Christ and belonging to him and to one another, proclaiming 'This is the faith of the church.'

➤**B8**

➤**E3**

The way the Church's initiation services are understood

For the national church there will be implications for the way its services of baptism (and associated services, such as confirmation) are structured and understood. The Church of England's *Common Worship* initiation services reflect this baptism-focused approach. Baptism is seen as the focus of Christian initiation. All the other services, such as Confirmation, Affirmation of Baptismal Faith, and Reception into the Communion of the Church of England, are seen as opportunities to enter further into the reality of baptism. They are pastoral rites which point back to the foundation event of baptism, and represent a further 'unpacking' or 'entering into' all that baptism represents. Indeed, in *CW Christian Initiation*, services of Reconciliation and Wholeness and Healing are also seen as, in some way, further stages in recovering or appropriating our baptism as our life circumstances change.

Ministry and service

Will you seek and serve Christ in all people,
loving your neighbour as yourself?
With the help of God, I will.

Question at the Commission,
CWCI, page 91

For the whole Church, baptism is a call to mission and service. Baptism is the call and commissioning of God's people for ministry in both the Church and the world. This means that any ministry (whether it is 'secular' work, locally appointed responsibility in the church, ordained ministry, or any other form of serving others), is a particular outworking of the call to play our part among God's people, which originates in baptism. All who are baptized are called to minister in one way or another, and when we commission or affirm a particular group in their ministry (whether that be children's workers, teachers, clergy or business people) we do so, conscious that this particular ministry is an outworking of baptism for these people and is only part of the ministry of all the baptized.

Mission and evangelism

Will you proclaim by word and example
the good news of God in Christ?
With the help of God, I will.

Question at the Commission,
CWCI, page 91

The 'ministry' to which all the baptized are called will include the responsibility for sharing our faith with others.

The biblical pictures of turning around on life's journey, of new creation and new birth (James 3.3ff; 1 Peter 1.12; James 1.18), imply new goals, new outlooks, new friends, new purposes. If this change in direction is to mean anything, it must at least involve a longing for others to make the same journey and for accompanying them on it. And because baptism is itself the welcome of new Christians, it reminds the whole Church that having new members should be normal, not exceptional. ➛

A5, A6, B1, B2 ➛

Baptism is thus both the motivation for mission and one of the means by which the Church engages in its missionary task. The fact that we often think about evangelism and nurture without being clear how baptism fits in shows that we have failed to make that connection.

'The renewal of baptismal practice is an integral part of mission and evangelism. In these services the whole Church is challenged to engage in generosity and seriousness with all those who are seeking new life in Christ.'

CWCI, page 9

But connecting baptism and evangelism means more than waiting for 'christening' enquirers to knock on our door and then making sure that our response is seen as part of our mission (though, hopefully it will be) - it will also mean being pro-active in laying before the wider community all that knowing Christ can mean and all that the Church offers - including the path to baptism and growth beyond it. It will involve church members in finding opportunities and being prepared to talk about their own baptism or subsequent journey of faith, both as individuals and as part of a group perhaps accompanying others on a similar journey. ➛

E1, E2, E4, E6 ➛

Living as God's holy people

When Martin Luther was tempted he said 'baptizatus sum' – 'I am baptized'. To sin willingly was unthinkable for someone who was 'in Christ' and, for him, there was no better way to sum up the fact that he was in Christ than to think of himself as a baptized person.

Sometimes it is the Church as a community which is faced with ethical dilemmas for which it needs the same clarity of thought and action. Sometimes the clear adversarial categories of black-white, alive-dead, light-darkness will not suffice, and in exploring the grey areas of decision-making both individual and Church will need the mind of Christ, full of compassion, and the discernment of the Spirit. But the very turning from and to, which is at the heart of baptism, reminds us that there are choices to be made, paths to be followed, and others to be avoided.

Letting baptism do its shaping

It would be possible – and might be an exciting exercise for the Church to undertake in a review or teaching course on baptism – to look at every single thing the Church does and ask, 'How does our baptism make a difference to what we do here?'

Does baptism make a difference to the relationships on the church council, or to its agenda? Are there underlying differences to the way the Church prays together, either as a whole, in small groups, pairs or as individuals, brought out by focusing on baptism? And what are the implications for putting baptism at the centre of the church's relationships with the wider local community? ➤

Does it, for instance, speak of separation from the wider world, or is it, like Jesus' baptism, a symbol of identification with humanity and its needs? Does it speak of a commitment to the local community as the baptismal imperatives of mission, service and ethics are worked out in practical terms? The way in which the local church manifests itself within the local community, whether by its notice boards, articles in the local paper, its jumble sales, its reputation for loving care of those at the bottom of society's heap – all are affected when the church is doing its baptismal theology.

And there is no better way to do baptismal theology than to do baptism – and to reflect on the doing to make sure that the integrity between sacrament and life which should be present is indeed present. The rest of this book aims to help in that task.

Do you renounce the deceit and corruption of evil?
I renounce them …

Do you submit to Christ as Lord?
I submit to Christ.

From the Decision, *CWCI*, page 67

**May the Father of all mercies
cleanse us from our sins
and restore us in his image
to the praise and glory of his
name,
through Jesus Christ our Lord.
Amen.**

An absolution from *Common Worship:
A Service of the Word*

➤**B11**

Questions for discussion

1. As an individual, when was the last time you consciously thought of yourself as a 'baptized person'?

2. Do you think it is possible to be a church that is shaped by baptism without realizing it, or does it have to be a conscious decision?

3. Can you think of areas of your church's life in which being a community of the baptized is making a difference? Are there areas where you think it could make more of a difference?

Who is asking for baptism today?

It was once thought that the Church of England baptized all the children of the nation (except for those of another denomination or religion). If this ever was the case, it is certainly not true today. It is not just that our society now includes more people of other faiths; among the vast majority of the population who would still think of themselves as (at least nominally) 'Christian' there has also been a shift in attitude and practice. There has been a decline in the number of parents coming to have babies and young children christened, and an increase in the number of people being baptized as young people or adults.

The situation is complex and varies from one part of the country to another. For instance, there is a division between the town and countryside, with the highest percentage of baptisms occurring in rural dioceses (Carlisle, Hereford and Lincoln). But there are also divisions between north and south, with Manchester having more baptisms than London. Some of the official church statistics are illustrated in the map (Fig. A1).

Some figures

In 1900 the Church of England baptized 650 infants for every 1,000 births. In 2000 the figure had fallen to 198 infants (under one year old) for every thousand births. In 1900 there were a total of 11,000 baptisms of older children and adults. By 2004 there were 37,900 children aged one to twelve baptized, and 8,300 adults. London has the lowest rate of baptism of infants, 53 per thousand births. Carlisle has the highest rate of baptism of infants, 412 per thousand births.

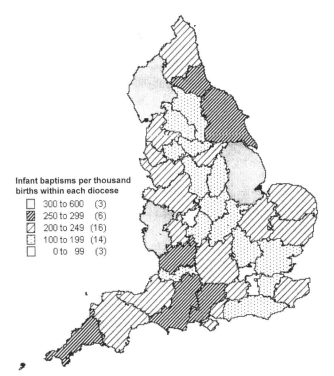

Infant baptisms per thousand births within each diocese

☐	300 to 600	(3)
▨	250 to 299	(6)
▨	200 to 249	(16)
▦	100 to 199	(14)
☐	0 to 99	(3)

Fig. A1: Infant baptisms in 2002

From *Church Statistics 2002*, Church House Publishing, 2004

The present situation

The Smiths

Mrs Smith got involved with her local church through a parent and toddler group. She got to know the people and began to go to the family service. Later on, her husband joined a beginners' group and their faith blossomed. She asked about getting the children baptized, but found out she had not been baptized herself. Now the whole family is preparing for baptism.

Fewer than 20 per cent of infants are baptized today. Many of the families represented by this proportion will be those who have had some church connection in the past and are open to the Church's message and to the idea of getting involved again – what the writers of *Mission-shaped Church* (Church House Publishing, 2004) refer to as 'open de-churched'.

These are the people who are most likely to come to the Church *asking* for baptism, and the report, *Mission-shaped Church,* suggests that this group is a key group with whom the Church can constructively engage. Some priority ought to be given to their inclusion and formation.

This leaves a vast section of the population who may well say they believe in God, tick a box to say they are a Christian (72 per cent of the population did so at the last census), or assert that they belong to the Church of England, but are not baptized. These people will have had no church involvement themselves in the past, and may come from families that have not been in regular contact with the Church for several generations. Baptism will not have been part of the family tradition for decades. They are what *Mission-shaped Church* calls 'non-churched'.

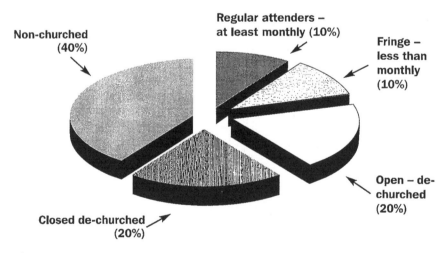

Fig. A2: Current or previous church involvement

From *Mission-shaped Church* © The Archbishops' Council (based on Philip Richter and Leslie Francis, *Gone but not Forgotten*, Darton, Longman & Todd, 1998), page 37.

These people are much less likely to come to the church asking for baptism for themselves or their children, and so the church will need to find other ways to establish initial contact with them. Links are likely to develop at first through 'mission' more generally, including all sorts of project work and evangelism. Any parish church involved in this sort of outreach will have plenty of adults (and their children) who will only begin to ask questions about baptism when they come to faith. They will need much more basic preparation than the open de-churched.➤ **➤C1**

Fresh expressions – breaking boundaries?

New expressions of church may begin to work less predictably, reaching people across the groups, including the open de-churched, the closed de-churched and the non-churched. The place of baptism in these churches (and the way it can connect them to the wider church) will have to be reviewed over the coming years.

The chapters that follow are written with this in mind, although the experiences drawn on are more directly from traditional expressions of church.

Questions for discussion

1. Who are the people that you have most contact with for mission? Are they more like the de-churched group or the non-churched group mentioned in this chapter? What are the implications of this?

2. Much Church of England thinking about baptism and mission has focused on the church responding to 'christening' requests from non-churchgoers. How could your church develop a strategy for mission and baptism that is more pro-active?

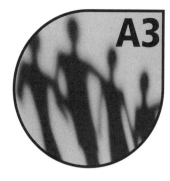

A3 Four journeys

One of the main aims of this book is to strengthen the interface between the Church and those who encounter it at varying stages in their journey of faith. It is useful to start with some stories based on real people and real events. These diverse accounts illustrate the ways people can meet and be touched by God. Each story is very different and calls for a different pastoral approach, different types of preparation. A chart is provided for each story, showing something of the process involved, and providing links from the stories and these different experiences of Christian initiation to other sections of the book. It is hoped that this will provide a useful way in to the material in the whole book.

Wayne and his family

B1➤ Veronica and Donald came to see Hazel the vicar two months before Wayne was born, ➤ wanting to set the date for a baptism. Hazel hadn't seen the couple before at church; gentle questioning revealed that Veronica's previous pregnancy had ended in a miscarriage, and now the couple wanted to seek peace with God by arranging a baptism in advance.

Hazel spent some time reassuring Veronica and Donald of God's love, and explained that they would be welcome to bring their baby to church for a service of Thanksgiving for the Gift of a Child as soon as convenient after the birth. 'However,' said Hazel, 'baptism involves making some serious promises about bringing your child up to follow Jesus. If you come to the course that I'm running, you'll find out what it's all about.'

B4, D2➤ Wayne was born, and they brought him to church for a public Thanksgiving service ➤ just ten days later. Veronica and Donald came to the course every week for two months. Much of what they learnt was familiar to Veronica because she had been confirmed as a teenager. Donald, however, hadn't been inside a church since his own baptism as a baby. He was meeting lots of new ideas on the course, and was more argumentative than the other seven people put together. The family started coming to church on Sunday about once a fortnight.

When Hazel showed Veronica and Donald the questions and promises in the baptism service, they said that they wanted to go ahead with it. But when Hazel asked Donald whether he wanted to
A6➤ be confirmed, he said that he didn't feel ready. ➤

Wayne was baptized at a Sunday service when he was three months old, and the church was packed with his parents' friends and relatives. Two of Wayne's godparents were old friends of Veronica and Donald, ► but the third was a new friend they had made at church. Everybody liked it when Hazel walked around the church with the newly baptized Wayne, though they weren't so sure about the bit when she splashed everyone with water from the font.►

►**C3, B7**

►**D7**

Donald and Veronica had been married, a couple of years before, in a register office with just a few friends present, so this well-attended service, and the reception in a local pub afterwards, felt like a public celebration of their marriage as well as the baptism.

Veronica started taking Wayne to a midweek meeting where parents studied the Bible while babies and tots were looked after.►

►**E2**

A few months later Donald said to Hazel that he had started praying at 'odd times of the day' and he felt ready to make the commitment of confirmation. A few weeks later he was confirmed at a service in the cathedral, and the following Sunday he was presented with his certificate at the Sunday service.►

►**B3**

Donald missed the discussions about God that he had enjoyed on the course – but soon found a church home group where he felt at home.

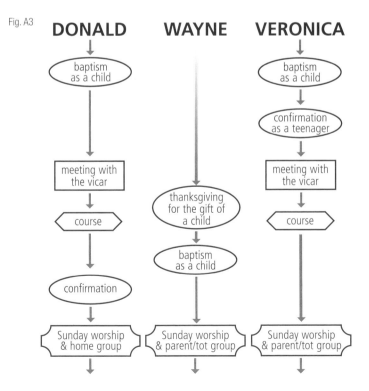

Fig. A3

DONALD — baptism as a child → meeting with the vicar → course → confirmation → Sunday worship & home group

WAYNE — thanksgiving for the gift of a child → baptism as a child → Sunday worship & parent/tot group

VERONICA — baptism as a child → confirmation as a teenager → meeting with the vicar → course → Sunday worship & parent/tot group

► **B1** Initial contacts
► **B4, D2** Thanksgiving
► **C2** Preparing a family for Christian baptism
► **D10** How to baptize

► **A6** What is confirmation?
   D12 Confirmation in practice

► **E1** The end – or just the beginning?

Phil and Sara

CW Christian Initiation includes some of the resources for Wholeness and Healing (including the Celebration of Wholeness and Healing service) from *CW Pastoral Services*. These are in the fourth section of the book, along with other means of 'recovering baptism' – that is, calling on God to make good or fulfil the promises of freedom and new creation contained in baptism. [E5]

See the Commentary section, *CWCI*, pages 351–4

Phil came to see Mike the curate because of the secondary cancer that had been found in his throat. His consultant had advised cancelling a foreign holiday that had already been booked, as he thought that Phil had only a few months to live. Phil said that he wanted to get right with God but didn't know what to do.

Mike didn't know Phil, but had met his sister Sara, who helped with the local Scouts, and came to church when it was parade Sunday.

Mike talked about God's love, shown by the death of Jesus on the cross for us, and the importance of trusting in him. Phil hadn't heard the cross explained in this way before – but he said that he would trust in God and accept whatever he wanted to give him.

Mike prayed for Phil, for wholeness and healing, and invited him to join a course that he was about to run, which could lead to baptism and confirmation – and perhaps Sara would like to come too?

C1➡ The next parade Sunday, Phil came to church with Sara and the Scouts, and the two of them came along to the ➡ weekly course. They got on well with Mike and the other people – and said that the course gave them a whole new way of looking at the world. Phil said that he now felt less stressed at work, and at peace about his cancer. Sara said that praying made her more patient with the Scouts.

B7➡ Phil and Sara were each linked up with another church member – a sponsor who ➡ befriended them, made them welcome at church, and prayed for them.

[See *CWCI*, pages 40-47] As the course went on, Phil and Sara and the others were presented with cards in church, each card bearing one of four key texts relevant to the Christian life: Jesus' Summary of the Law, the Lord's Prayer, the Apostles' Creed and the Beatitudes.

D10➡
D13➡
E3➡
Sara knew that she had been baptized as a child, but Phil had no record of his baptism, and his few living relatives had conflicting memories. So Mike gave Phil a conditional baptism, by immersion in a tank that the church hired for the event. ➡ Sara didn't want to be left out, so she ➡ affirmed her baptismal vows, with water, at the same time. ➡ Although it wasn't a parade Sunday, lots of the Scouts came to witness the spectacle!

A6➡ When the next deanery confirmation took place a couple of months later, Phil and Sara were both confirmed ➡.

At his next clinic, Phil's consultant was amazed to find how well his cancer was responding to treatment, and said that overseas holidays could be considered again.

Phil and Sara remained regular in attendance at church on Sundays. Phil joined the monthly men's breakfast group, of which his sponsor was already a member. Sara tried joining the weekly homegroup of her sponsor, but soon realised that she didn't have enough time to spare for this. Later on though, her sponsor took Sara to an annual Christian conference/holiday, which became a regular fixture in her diary. ☛

☛**E2**

Fig. A4

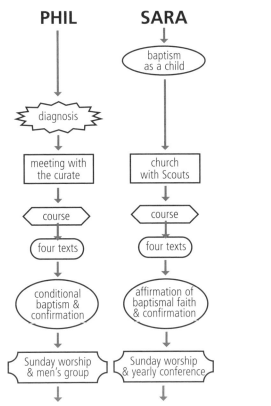

☛ **A1** A Church shaped by baptism

☛ **C1** Preparing adults for baptism
☛ **C5** Preparing for confirmation

☛ **D3** Baptism service structure
☛ **D10** How to baptize
☛ **D12** Confirmation in practice
☛ **D13** Affirmation and Reception

☛ **E1** The end – or just the beginning?

Musa

Musa came from Nigeria, son of an Anglican mother and a Muslim father. Although his mother had died when he was ten years old, his father said that he was free to choose the faith that he wanted. While he was a student in Lagos, he took part in an Alpha course, run by a Baptist church, and he decided to make Jesus the Lord of his life. However, he hesitated to get baptized, because to his father and Muslim friends that would be seen as a permanent rejection of Islam.

When Musa came to a British university to study for a second degree, he went with a friend on his course to a mid-week café event run by Christians, with music, Bible study and open discussion. After the first term, he approached the university's Anglican chaplain, Ron, and asked to be baptized. Ron knew that Musa had learnt a lot from Alpha, and from the Christian café. Rather than make Musa follow a preparation course, Ron gave Musa a book to study, and met with him for three evenings, to fill some of the gaps in his knowledge. Ron asked another student, also from Africa, to meet regularly with Musa, to pray with him and act as his sponsor

B7 ➤ ➤ on the Christian journey. At each of four café evenings, Musa was presented with one of the key texts after a short multimedia

C1 ➤ presentation based on the text itself. ➤ On the fifth Thursday Musa was baptized at the café, and everyone learnt a couple of Nigerian worship songs. Some of Musa's flatmates came, and were stunned that something religious could feel so good.

Ron raised the possibility of confirmation, but didn't push it. Musa didn't know which denomination he would join back in Nigeria, but in

Fig. A5

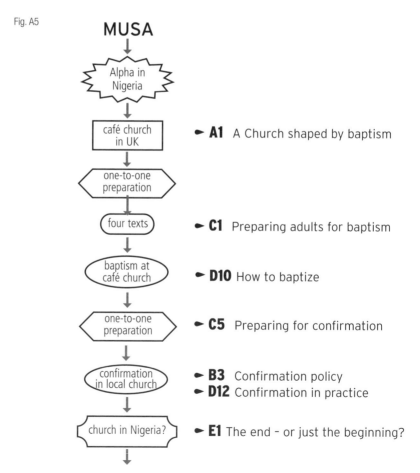

MUSA

Alpha in Nigeria

café church in UK — **A1** A Church shaped by baptism

one-to-one preparation

four texts — **C1** Preparing adults for baptism

baptism at café church — **D10** How to baptize

one-to-one preparation — **C5** Preparing for confirmation

confirmation in local church — **B3** Confirmation policy
— **D12** Confirmation in practice

church in Nigeria? — **E1** The end - or just the beginning?

the end was convinced by some friends that he might as well be ready to be Anglican there. ➨ So after a couple more preparation sessions, he was confirmed at a church near the university, when the Bishop came there. ➨**A6**

Musa said, 'I am glad to have made this public commitment. Before I was baptized I felt a fraud when I was talking with my flatmates about my faith, but now I am a true witness.' ➨ ➨**E4**

Emma and her Grandma

Emma was eight years old when Mark the vicar started visiting her primary school. She was intrigued by his stories, and asked at home if she could start going to Sunday school at church. Her Grandma said she was willing to take her each week. So Emma and Grandma went along to St John's. After a few months Emma started asking Grandma questions about baptism. Had she been baptized? Why not? Could she be? So Grandma and Emma spoke to Mark, and he came to visit the family. Emma's parents had no objection – after all, they had left the whole question of having Emma christened because they wanted her to make up her own mind, and now she had done.

Mark, Emma, and her parents and Grandma prepared for the service together. ➨ Emma was quite clear that she wanted to be baptized by going under the water, not by being splashed. She also helped to choose her godparents, one of them being Grandma and another being a new friend from the church. ➨**C2**

The big day came, and Emma made her promises in a strong voice, and was baptized by submersion.➨ ➨**D10**

Soon after this, Mark gave Emma, and some other children who came to church, a short series of lessons about Holy Communion. ➨ They were admitted to Communion at another special Sunday service.➨ ➨**C4** ➨**D11**

Since then her parents have been coming to church from time to time as well, and her mother has begun to talk about being confirmed.

At school Emma has been sharing her enthusiasm for Jesus with her friends, and they are going to start a lunch-time Bible club.➨ ➨**E4**

Fig. A6

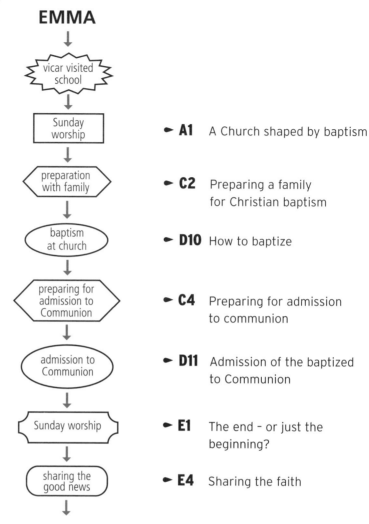

EMMA

Flow	Reference	Description
vicar visited school		
Sunday worship	**A1**	A Church shaped by baptism
preparation with family	**C2**	Preparing a family for Christian baptism
baptism at church	**D10**	How to baptize
preparing for admission to Communion	**C4**	Preparing for admission to communion
admission to Communion	**D11**	Admission of the baptized to Communion
Sunday worship	**E1**	The end - or just the beginning?
sharing the good news	**E4**	Sharing the faith

Questions for discussion

1. Looking at each story, at what point would you say that each person became a Christian?

2. Would your church have welcomed these people in a different way?

3. How would you want to follow up each person, and encourage them to grow more in Christ?

What is baptism?

The day of Pentecost

After Jesus rose from the dead and ascended into heaven, his disciples stayed together as a community in Jerusalem. Jesus had told them to await the coming of the Holy Spirit. That promise was fulfilled at the Feast of Pentecost (fifty days from Passover, when Jesus was crucified): the Holy Spirit came upon them with power. Immediately they were out in the street full of the good news, and Peter preached to the crowds (many of them there on pilgrimage) about Jesus and his death and resurrection. The account in the book of Acts shows how the people responded, wanting to know what to do – and were then told the 'way in' was through repenting and being baptized 'in the name of Jesus Christ'.

From God's point of view, as people came to baptism they were being incorporated in the Church which he was bringing to birth that day. From their point of view the baptism involved a true commitment to Jesus Christ; and the seriousness of that commitment was shown by their way of life – they devoted themselves 'to the apostles' teaching and fellowship'. In other words, they both *believed* and *belonged*.

That is Christian baptism. It has been from that day to this. Men and women alike met with Jesus Christ, as they came to believe he was alive from the dead. Many of them would not have known him when he was on earth, and others had only 'known' him in the sense that they had called for his death before Pilate. They repented – that is to say, they left their previous way of life – and belonged now with the apostles and the growing community gathered round them. They were now disciples, living not for themselves, but with the living Lord Jesus in charge of their lives.

Today, baptism is still the same 'way in' to the same pattern of living as disciples of Jesus. It separates people from the old life and joins them to the Church, the actual company of believers.

'Now when they heard this, they were cut to the heart and said to Peter and to the other apostles, "Brothers, what should we do?" Peter said to them: "Repent, and be baptized every one of you in the name of Jesus Christ so that your sins may be forgiven; and you will receive the gift of the Holy Spirit. For the promise is for you, for your children, and for all who are far away, everyone whom the Lord our God calls to him"... So those who welcomed his message were baptized and that day about three thousand persons were added. They devoted themselves to the apostles' teaching and fellowship, to the breaking of bread and the prayers.'

Acts 2.37-39, 41-42

So what does Christian baptism mean?

Baptism was not a completely new idea on the day of Pentecost. John the Baptist, second cousin to Jesus, had been the advance messenger and herald of Jesus' coming, and had prepared people with a 'baptism of repentance' in the river Jordan.

'John the Baptist appeared in the wilderness of Judea, proclaiming: "Repent, for the kingdom of heaven has come near" . . . Then the people of Jerusalem and all Judea were going out to him, and all the region along the Jordan, and they were baptized by him in the river Jordan, confessing their sins.'

Matthew 3.1-2, 5-6

John's baptism had been in preparation, looking forward to the coming of the Messiah, and to the gift of the Holy Spirit. Baptism may have been a new idea, but it is more likely that it already existed and was used in bringing Gentiles into Judaism as converts ('proselyte baptism') - for it could be given to women, which circumcision could not. So the scandal of John's baptism was that this ceremony of repentance and cleansing was now being urged not upon the 'unclean' Gentiles, but upon the 'holy' people of God. Repentance and cleansing had to begin with the Jews, for Jesus the Messiah was coming first to them.

'Go therefore and make disciples of all nations, baptizing them in the name of the Father and of the Son and of the Holy Spirit, and teaching them to obey everything that I have commanded you.'

Matthew 28.19-20

This sign of cleansing and repentance (and much more) was what Jesus then commanded his followers to continue after his resurrection, as part of the process for welcoming people of all the earth into the company of his disciples. It looks as though they were to preach not only repentance and the importance of following the way of life that Jesus commanded, but also both *faith* in the Father, Son and Holy Spirit, and also *baptism* in their name.

This is almost exactly what we found the followers of Jesus doing on the Day of Pentecost. Baptism meant being joined to God in order to live the life that Jesus had commanded. And in baptizing new converts Jesus' followers were forming a company of believers - the Church.

See the table on page 323 for the huge range of overlapping biblical imagery which has informed the words and imagery of the CW baptism service.

Actually, everything involved in conversion was signified in baptism. There are other New Testament texts about belonging to Christ in his death and resurrection, about being baptized 'by the Holy Spirit into one body', about 'putting on Christ' as a garment, and about 'walking in newness of life.' According to the New Testament, baptism ushers in the lot.

> ## A theological framework
> In preparing these services and additional supporting rites the Liturgical Commission had before it the following biblical framework, believing that baptism involves:
> ¶ *separation* from this world – that is, the world alienated from God, and
> ¶ *reception* into a universal community centred on God, within which
> ¶ his children can *grow* into the fullness of the pattern of Christ, and
> ¶ a community whose *mission* is to serve God's Spirit in redeeming the world.
>
> Page 319

Learning what it means to be a baptized believer

When the apostle Paul, in his letters, mentions baptism and what it means for believers, he is telling his readers what it means for them that they are baptized people. He is not asking them whether they *remember* their baptism. They may have a good recall, or they may not. Perhaps some of them had been baptized as infants ➤ and would certainly not remember their baptism. No, what is happening is that Paul is treating them as, here and now, baptized people (just as you can treat people – and he in his letters did – as 'married' without every time expecting them to think back to their actual marriage ceremony). And each time what he is saying is, 'Baptism is into Christ - you are incorporated as a member of Christ - this is how those who are baptized into Christ should live.'

... and baptism is once-for-all-for-life

Because Paul can say, years after someone's baptism, 'You are baptized', it is obvious it only needs to happen once. It does not wear out or wear off. Even though you cannot see someone is baptized, it is 'there' in that person's life, like an internal tattoo. This makes it quite important to be sure that a baptism really was a baptism, and to keep records in a baptismal register and issue certificates to those who get baptized. In addition, the Church of England (and other churches) also offer services of thanksgiving (or blessing, or dedication) for babies and young children, which do not involve water and are not baptism. This makes it important to know what is *not* baptism, as well as what is, so that someone who has had one of these services as a baby, knows in the future that they can still be a candidate for baptism.

➤**A5**

Is 'in the name of Jesus Christ' (Acts 2) in conflict with 'into the name of the Father and of the Son and of the Holy Spirit' (Matthew 28)? No, for it is likely they were not meant to be formulae, but simply to give the meaning of baptism – and both meanings fit.

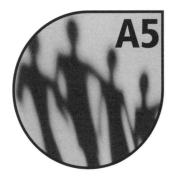

Why baptize infants?

Is it right to baptize infants, or very young children? The question emerges quite quickly from this starting point: that the pattern of baptism used by both John the Baptist and the various church leaders in the Acts of the Apostles involves repentance and faith. It is a bit difficult, so the argument goes, at least at first sight, to attribute either repentance or faith to the three-week-old child.

One section of the Christian Church would answer 'no', because those children will not be able to express their own repentance and faith in any credible way. So, that section of the Church would say, it would be better – or even necessary – to wait for the time they can make a credible profession of faith for themselves. Many deny that the baptism of an infant is a baptism at all, and they will give a 'believer's baptism' to grown converts, even those already baptized years before in infancy.

'Jesus said: "Let the little children come to me, and do not stop them."'

Matthew 19.14

This might be a good argument for a service of Thanksgiving for the Gift of a Child, but is too remote from baptism to carry force in the argument about baptism of infants.

Initially the case above looks fairly plausible, and many Christians accept it. But actually Scripture gives ample warrant for baptizing the newborn children of Christians; this practice fits closely with the way the children are to be brought up; and delaying baptism in Christian families may create more problems than it solves (for more on this see the end of this section).

What do we find about children in Judaism at the time Jesus was on earth? Well, they were included in their religion with the parents and older children. The boys were circumcised straight after birth, and children had their part in the passover feast, the synagogue, the sabbath, and the pilgrim visits to Jerusalem. They simply belonged in the Jewish family and in the larger community. But what was the significance of male circumcision, and what has this got to do with baptism today?

'Both the slave born in your house and the one bought with your money must be circumcised. So shall my covenant be in your flesh an everlasting covenant.'

Genesis 17.13

'. . . a son . . . Isaac. I will establish my covenant with him as an everlasting covenant.'

Genesis 17.19

The Old Testament circumcision

Male circumcision was the mark that distinguished the tribes of Israel from the surrounding Gentile nations. Was it then simply a tribal marking, as children born into a tribe inevitably belonged to it, and were marked accordingly (and, we might note, irreversibly)?

No, in origin circumcision was *not* simply a tribal or national sign. In the first two generations it was given to Ishmael and Isaac without distinction by Abraham, and (presumably) to Esau and Jacob without distinction by Isaac. It was a mark of the covenant God was making to create a people from the seed of Abraham; but it was given to both sons when there was no certainty, at the time of giving it, which son would be the true heir of the promise. Both sons were to be *treated as heirs,* until such time as it was clear that one of them was not.

When we get to the New Testament we find there is a commentary on this, as Paul reflects upon what Abraham did when circumcision began. He strives to make clear (over against Jewish belief) that it was not the circumcision itself that brought salvation to Abraham. Circumcision was a 'sign' of 'the righteousness that he had by faith'. But this is exactly what baptism is in the New Testament. And, although to Abraham his circumcision was a 'seal' of the righteousness he had already received from God, its basic meaning was to be a *sign* of that righteousness, and Abraham gave it to Isaac straight after birth. Would not an apostle who argues this way about circumcision equally expect to give baptism to both adults and their children on conversion? It may not be proof, but it begins a cumulative case.

For baptism to replace circumcision makes good sense; for it has the same initiatory character as circumcision and is given once for all for life (so that the recipients are then 'baptized' people). But note that it is given to men and women without distinction. Thus in the new covenant women belong to God and to his people not simply by being attached to men, but as redeemed people in their own right.

Proselyte baptism

We move on to another pointer towards children being baptized. If 'proselyte baptism' ☛ was indeed being practised by the time of John the Baptist, then this involved not only parents, but also their children (along with the boys being circumcised). In some English versions of the Bible, proselytes are called 'converts to Judaism', so they may be hard to pick out – but they are only mentioned four times in the New Testament, and one of those four times is on the day of Pentecost. So we are left with a question as to how the apostles treated them and their children.

If they had been baptized into Judaism as a whole family, and now learned that the heart of Judaism was Christ, and were urged to be baptized into his name, would they, or would they not, have retained a kind of corporate solidarity? Were the adults to become Jewish Christian believers, but the children to be left as Jewish children? It

'Then Abraham took his son Ishmael and . . . every male among the men of Abraham's household, and he circumcised the flesh of their foreskins that very day.'

Genesis 17.23

'We say, "Faith was reckoned to Abraham as righteousness." . . . Was it before or after he had been circumcised? It was not after, but before he was circumcised. He received the sign of circumcision as a seal of the righteousness that he had by faith while he was still uncircumcised.'

Romans 4.9-11

☛A4

'. . . residents of Mesopotamia, Judaea and Cappadocia, Pontus and Asia, Phrygia . . . and visitors from Rome, both Jews and proselytes . . . in our own languages we hear them speaking about God's deeds of power.'

Acts 2.9-11

does not clinch the point, but it is interesting that Peter actually mentions their children when responding to the question, 'Brothers, what shall we do?' His answer – that the promise is 'for you, for your children, and all who are far away' – can be read in two different ways:

'The promise is for you, for your children, and for all who are far away, everyone whom the Lord our God calls to him.'

Acts 2.39

- 'for you – and (in years ahead) your-children-and-all-(others)-who-are-far-away' or
- 'for you-and-your-children – and (in years ahead) all who are far away'.

Despite the uncertainty, there is a good starting point here for thinking that the New Testament Christians genuinely thought in 'household' terms with a family solidarity.

Household baptism

This would only be a pointer in the case for baptizing infants, and, if there were no further signposts pointing in the same direction, it might rank as insubstantial. However, in a quite artless way, the idea of households turning to Christ comes along at intervals in the New Testament and provides further evidence.

There is a key word for this – in the Greek letters it is *oikos*. *Oikos* means a 'house' with the same breadth of meaning as 'house' has in English. For us it can mean simply the building, or it can mean a community, whether that is a nuclear family, or a college, or whatever. It is the same in the New Testament. In Acts 2 it means a house or home in verse 46, but it quite often means a 'household', and sometimes it means a household at the very point of conversion, indeed a household being *baptized as a household*.

The *oikos* word comes to us in English particularly in the original meaning of a word like 'economy' (the principle of running a household – *nomos* is Greek for a law or principle).

Peter, when he had baptized the Gentiles in Cornelius' home (Acts 10.44-48), reported it thus:

'. . . [Cornelius] had seen [an] angel . . . saying "Send to Joppa and bring Simon, who is called Peter; he will give you a message by which you and all your household will be saved."'

Acts 11.13-14

There are five specific instances in the New Testament which look as though they might be 'household baptism'. Of course, none of them mentions that there were children (let alone babes in arms) present, but together they present a powerful case for treating the family, including children, as a unit. Indeed, if there were any reason to think that children under a certain age, or not able to profess their faith personally, were present but *not* baptized, then if words like 'the whole household' were being used, the exceptions would have needed stating.

The five instances include the first Gentiles, the first converts in Europe, and both a Jewish and a Gentile family in Corinth. In each case the word *oikos* occurs, and baptisms are reported (or, alternatively, that only those who 'heard' and 'believed' the word were baptized). The first four are recorded in the Acts of the Apostles, and amount to a high proportion of the nine different occasions of baptism recorded in the Acts. Of the other five, the initial one on the day of Pentecost is discussed in section A4 above; two more are clearly individuals out on their own (the eunuch in the desert in Acts 8, and Saul after his Damascus Road experience in Acts 9); and only two other occurrences remain (the Samaritans in Acts 8, and the group which knew only John's baptism in Acts 19). When seen in those terms, the mention of households is not exceptional but could be regarded as reflecting what was natural and normal.

A household may well have included more than family members. Slaves may have been included. Lydia, the seller of purple, had a household of which she was the head. She may have been a widow, or even a single woman; her household may have been children, or slaves, or others – or a combination. At any rate, she had a household, and the whole household was baptized.

The other households read as though they belonged to a married man with a family. And it is worth noting that, despite statements that are sometimes made, there really was a nuclear family of parents and children in the New Testament. A very good illustration comes in Ephesians 5 and 6, where husband and wife are to love each other (chapter 5) and parents and children have mutual responsibilities towards each other (6.1-4). They discharge them 'in the Lord' and 'in the discipline of the Lord'. The case is strong that parents treated their children as 'in the Lord' with them – but then anyone being treated as 'in the Lord' was surely baptized?

Contemporary practice

So what action is to be taken today for the child of believers? Unless he or she is baptized soon after birth, then Paul's assumption that a Christian is a baptized person loses its impact. A later baptism would not begin the Christian life, but mark a stage of growth within it.

In the Church of England today, *Christian Initiation* simply assumes that there will be occasions when parents and children will be baptized together. Note 8 (page 99) says that the questions can be answered in the form 'We reject . . .'. The Commentary suggests (page 343) the use of the short version of the Commission for use when children are able to answer for themselves.

Lydia in Philippi, reported like this:

'When she and her household were baptized.'

Acts 16.15

The **Philippian jailer**'s story, following the earthquake:

'They said to him "Believe on the Lord Jesus Christ and you will be saved and so will your household." Then they spoke the word of the Lord to him and to all who were in his house . . . and he was himself baptized and so were all his immediately . . . and he rejoiced whole-household-wise, believing in the Lord.'

Acts 16.31-34 (Contributor's translation)

A possible witness is **Crispus** in Corinth:

'Crispus, the official of the synagogue, became a believer in the Lord, together with all his household; and many of the Corinthians who heard Paul became believers and were baptized.'

Acts 18.8

When **Paul** writes to Corinth he says

'I baptized none of you except Crispus and Gaius . . . (I did baptize also the household of Stephanas).'

1 Corinthians 1.14-16

In many parts of Africa where the church is growing, it is quite usual for parents to choose together to follow Christ, and bring their children of various ages with them for baptism. In Congo, for example, the old Swahili prayer book used to have different services for the baptism of children and the baptism of adults; but the revised prayer book printed in 1998 combined these into one service for all, as much for convenience as to say that adult and infant baptism are the same thing.

Some guidelines for parents today

We do not know each others' hearts. Our decision to treat each other as believers or unbelievers depends upon some rule of thumb. Thus people who attend worship tend to be treated as believers. In the New Testament *baptism* marks the boundary of the visible church, where the baptized are treated as believers. The unbaptized are unbelievers, until they profess belief, at which point they are immediately baptized.

So how are believers to treat their own children? Those who do not baptize their infants in formal terms state 'my children are born as unbelievers and do not belong to any circle of believers until they have an identifiable conversion at an age where their profession of faith is credible'. But, in practice, few Christian parents actually behave that way – on the contrary: they are more likely to teach their children to say 'Our Father' and mean it, and to read them Bible stories as if they already applied to them. But, if so, should not such parents treat their children consistently as believers, and mark them as such in the water of baptism, and include them formally in the life of the church? Surely a child, in a home where Christ is known, should, on meeting peers in pre-school or kindergarten friendships, discover that there are children out there trying to live life without Jesus? That is surely why Paul tells parents to 'bring the children up *in* the discipline and instruction of the Lord' (Ephesians 6.4)? That 'in' is significant.

Some limits?

Infant baptism is securely based in the New Testament *for the children of believers*. The New Testament, however, gives no basis for baptizing children in households *without* Christian faith. Indeed, if such children do eventually come to faith in Jesus Christ, it might be better if their baptism came as part of that later conversion.

Though a case can be made for baptizing such children in infancy (and this is envisaged under some approaches outlined in Section B2), it does nevertheless have two disadvantages:

- first, it can mislead all concerned at the time of the baptism itself; and
- secondly, because baptism is given only once for life, it deprives the children of a very meaningful and wonderful rite of passage when they do become believers later.

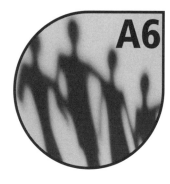

A6

What is confirmation?

'The Western Church, and to this day the Church of England, uses the term 'confirmation' in different and often overlapping senses. It has been applied to different parts of the process of incorporation into Christ:

¶ *To establish or secure.* This is the earliest and non-technical sense. It is used of an action in which the Church accepts and acts on baptism. It was applied to the first receiving of communion as well as to episcopal anointing and hand-laying.

¶ *A post-baptismal episcopal rite.* In the ninth century this technical sense attaches itself to the exclusively Western practice of a post-baptismal episcopal rite. There has been a continuing debate in the West as to whether this 'confirmation' consists of the general prayer for the sevenfold gift of the Spirit said over all the candidates or of the specific act of praying for each candidate that follows the general prayer.

¶ *To strengthen.* This understanding of the episcopal rite became widespread in the thirteenth century, having been applied earlier to an adult's need of strength to witness and to resist temptation, and then transferred to children as they approach adulthood.

¶ *To approve or recognize.* In Cranmer's rites the bishop's action is seen as signifying the Church's recognition of the personal faith nurtured in the catechetical process.

¶ *To ratify.* The meaning of individual or personal ratification emerges in the preface added to the confirmation service in *The Book of Common Prayer* (1662).'

CW Chistian Initiation, Commentary, pages 346–7.

This could sound like a recipe for confusion – just look at the history – but it also shows that, to an extent, confirmation can represent different things to different candidates. So it is very important both that the service is tailored to reflect the different understandings the candidates might have, and also that the candidates are well prepared with a broad knowledge of how their spiritual situation, and that of others, is met by the words of the service. ➤

D12 ➤

How can confirmation be used today?

Five possible scenarios might be:

- a way to affirm your growth to an adult faith (and adult church membership) if you were baptized as an infant and brought up within the church;

- a way to renew your commitment to Christ if you were baptized as an infant but drifted away from faith, and have now returned as an adult;

- an accompaniment to baptism for someone coming to adult faith with no church background;
- a way to join the Church of England from another church;
- a way to mark your admission to Holy Communion.

Affirming faith

Lucy grew up in a Christian home and was baptized as a baby. She went to Sunday school and to the Church youth group, and now she is 14 she is being confirmed. She has never known a time when she did not know Jesus and feel she was a Christian. She would not talk about having had a 'conversion experience' – but she knows she is a Christian and wants to be a follower of Jesus. She has never really had a chance to stand up in public and affirm her faith. For her, confirmation really will be confirming her faith and her baptism. Confirmation will also mark her entry into adult church life – she moves into the youth group from the Pathfinder group after confirmation. It is only one step towards adult membership, of course (because she cannot vote at the Annual Meeting or serve on the PCC until she is 17), but it is a significant step nonetheless.

Renewing commitment

Rob was baptized as a baby too, like Lucy, and even attended Junior Church for a few years, on and off. However, he stopped going to church when he was a teenager. At university he got to know some Christians who took him to church now and again, but it was when he left college and started work that he began to think about Christianity seriously again. A friend from his office invited him to an Alpha course and eventually he recommitted his life to Christ. Rob sometimes thinks this is when he became a Christian and sometimes he thinks he was a Christian when he was younger and has come back to his faith. In any case, confirmation gives him the chance to say he wants to be a Christian from now on.

Accompanying adult baptism

Carl never had any church involvement before he and his partner decided to have a church wedding. Something someone said at the marriage preparation sessions made him think about faith, and after joining the Emmaus course, he decided to become a Christian and be baptized. Some in the church felt that confirmation was unnecessary, as he would be making his own adult promises at his baptism, but the vicar encouraged him to see confirmation as a way of associating himself with the wider church, beyond this particular parish, through the involvement of the bishop in confirmation. He was baptized and confirmed in the same service, at the cathedral.

Joining the Church of England

Geoff and Marion have been members of the United Reformed Church (URC) but have moved to a village where the only church is the Anglican one, and they decided to get involved there. After a year or two they decided that they would probably be staying there for quite a while and would join the Church of England – the vicar talked to them at length about changing churches and especially about the distinctive differences between the Church of England and the URC. Since the URC does not have bishops (or confirmation), Geoff and Marion will be confirmed as the way of becoming Anglicans.

If Geoff and Marion had been members of a church that practises episcopal confirmation, such as the Roman Catholic Church, then the service of Reception would have been used instead. [D13]

Admission to Holy Communion

For centuries, confirmation has been, for Anglicans, the normal way of being admitted to Holy Communion. Recent changes mean that this no longer has to be the case, and many churches are moving to a pattern of admitting children to Holy Communion before confirmation. ◄ However, in a majority of parishes, admission to communion is still seen as a major part of what confirmation means.

B8, D11◄

Matt was baptized as a baby and is now being confirmed with several other 10-year-olds in his church. At the Confirmation service he will receive the bread and wine of Holy Communion for the first time and his confirmation classes have included quite a lot of teaching about the Eucharist.

'([the Samaritans] had only been baptized in the name of the Lord Jesus). Then Peter and John laid their hands on them, and they received the Holy Spirit.'

Acts 8.16-17

'When I was a schoolboy, about 15 years of age, the bishop coming into the country, many went to him to be confirmed: we that were boys ran out to see the bishop among the rest, not knowing anything of the meaning of the business . . . The bishop examined us not at all in one article of the faith; but in a church-yard, in haste we were set in a rank, and he passed hastily over us, laying his hand on our head and saying a few words which neither I nor any I spoke with, understood.'

Richard Baxter's confirmation, c. 1630

A bit of history

There are only three places in the New Testament where baptism in water is followed by laying-on of hands, including what looks like an emergency action in Acts 8. Otherwise, water baptism conveys full initiation.

- From around AD 200, baptism was often followed (within the same ceremony) by either laying on of hands or anointing with oil, with reference being made to the Holy Spirit.
- From AD 500, baptism and what was later called confirmation drift apart because of the requirement for babies to be baptized immediately after they were born, coupled with the difficulty of bishops not being able to travel around quickly. So the need arose for what became an infrequent service where vows were ratified and prayer was made for the candidates to be strengthened by the Spirit.
- At the Reformation in the Church of England, the service lost all reference to the Spirit and became a gateway to receiving Holy Communion after instruction through the catechism.

- Until the major development of the road and rail network in the nineteenth century, bishops still could not get round quickly enough, and stories of abuse abound, including fighting to get to the bishop. Reforming bishops sought to visit major centres in their dioceses once every three years. But the real change came with the popularization of a 'two-stage' doctrine of initiation in the 1890s, with confirmation by a bishop being identified with the gift of the Spirit and therefore essential to initiation.
- One result of this was 'the high pastoral profile of confirmation within the mission of the Church' which was 'largely a development of the nineteenth century' (Commentary, page 348). Another was the stimulation of continuing debate about the relationship of confirmation to admission to communion.

◄B8

Successive Lambeth Conferences have commended both the 'traditional' view of baptism followed by confirmation followed by communion, and different variants on allowing the baptized to take communion before confirmation. This might involve admission to communion 'at an appropriate age' after instruction, with confirmation later as a rite for young adults being commissioned for 'the task of being a Christian in society'; or it might involve administering infant baptism and confirmation together, as in the Orthodox churches, where confirmation is done by the presbyter and not the bishop. Episcopal commissioning comes later. The rites in *CW Christian Initiation* make 'no attempt to resolve these questions'. They are designed to be used by people following differing policies, though because '[o]n all views confirmation derives its meaning from baptism', '[t]he structure of the services . . . conforms carefully to that of the baptism service' (Commentary, page 348).

Questions for discussion

1. Which of the different elements of confirmation do you think has been most important in your church in the past?

2. Are there other aspects that need to be brought into clearer focus now?

3. How do people learn about the meaning of confirmation in your church (other than the candidates themselves)? Is there a need for some general teaching – and if so, how should it be delivered?

Gladstone described confirmations in York Minster by Archbishop Vernon Harcourt (1807–47): 'The nave would be filled with candidates from the surrounding towns and villages and the hubbub of talk would be stilled by vergers calling "Silence for the Archbishop!" His Grace would then appear and ascend a pulpit placed for the purpose. When the time came for the imposition of hands, the Archbishop, standing in the pulpit, would extend his hands over the whole multitude and repeat the words of Confirmation once, then the last prayers were said and the Archbishop withdrew, though he had not laid his hands on the head of a single candidate.'

Section

B

B1

POLICY
Initial contacts

A2, A3 ➤

We have already seen the complexity of the context in which the Church welcomes new members through baptism. We have also seen the variety of routes by which candidates of every age and stage come into contact with the Church. ➤ However, for most Church of England churches still, the biggest and most regular issue is how to respond to requests for *infant* baptism, as these often come from those with no regular church contact. In this section we start with a focus on one particular story as a foundation for looking at policy issues more broadly.

For many young parents, booking a 'christening' will be their first adult contact with the Church. For those who have been married in church, the baptism could be their first contact in a new parish. Most churches try to be friendly and welcoming, but sometimes we underestimate the distance between our best intentions and how it feels to be that parent making a tentative enquiry.

Laura's story

Dawn had just celebrated her first birthday. Laura, her mum, had just moved out of her own parental home, having been on a housing association waiting list for eighteen months. She hadn't told anybody who Dawn's father was. It had happened at a party and wasn't a liaison she was particularly proud of.

Laura's mum had been anxious for some time that Dawn hadn't been christened yet. Her own mother would be turning in her grave. But life had just been too chaotic.

Now that Laura had a place of her own and there was a little bit more space and organization, her mum had told her to make a booking with the church to have Dawn 'done' some time in the summer.

Laura had called at the vicarage but nobody was in. There was a phone number on the church notice board so she rang that but got an answer-phone. Not knowing what to say to the machine she had rung several more times before getting a real person. She had known there would be someone in at tea-time. The woman had been a bit abrupt on the phone but had told her to go to something she called a 'surgery' that was held round the back of the church hall on a Thursday night. In the meantime Laura had rung the local community centre and made a provisional booking to use it for a party to wet the baby's head on a Sunday afternoon in June. It took Laura a couple of weeks to pluck up the courage to go to the surgery. She wondered why a doctor needed to be there to book a christening. It was a wet night and a long walk. Dawn was a little fractious when they got there. Laura wasn't sure which door was the entrance. The main doors were all locked up. There was a small side door that was open a crack so she went through there. It wasn't easy getting the buggy up the steps.

When Laura got inside there was a young couple holding hands and filling some forms in with an old lady. She asked where she went to book a christening and was told she needed to sit down and wait.

Margaret had been churchwarden of St Richard's for 17 years. She had started looking after the parish surgery when the last-but-one vicar left, and the replacement had been perfectly happy for her to carry on. The new vicar had now been with them only a few months, and she had told him that this was her job. She could tell that Laura would be trouble the moment she saw her.

Twenty minutes later it was Laura's turn. Dawn was proving to be very crotchety and it was a bit of a struggle concentrating on what the lady was saying. Laura had never heard of a 'parish', but it seemed that she lived in a different one now, even though St Richard's had always been her church. She was going to have to see another vicar, but wasn't too sure which one. She also learnt that she might not be able to have the service on the Sunday she had booked the community centre for. The lady kept talking about baptisms anyhow, and Laura was sure that she only wanted Dawn christened.

As she left she decided that she probably wouldn't fit in at the church anyway and if she cancelled the community centre she would be able to afford a new television to keep Dawn occupied.

Welcome and clarity

There is inevitably scope for conflict when people with two different mindsets enter negotiations. This often happens when a family wanting 'the baby done' come to the church that only offers Christian baptism. Very deep injuries indeed can result if these negotiations are handled badly. On the other hand, these contacts present the church with fantastic opportunities to help people move from a vague and uncertain faith to greater maturity and deeper understanding.

The impressions formed by families who approach the church for a baptism will influence them greatly. These may be the first adult impressions of church that many receive. There is no reason why these shouldn't convey a good sense of a community that cares about individuals, that is open, welcoming and speaks the same language as the rest of the community. Every church needs to present a mature and thought-through faith that invites others to join the journey.

Christian people will see baptism as a sacrament of real significance and will want to avoid treating it lightly. Indeed, the World Council of Churches Faith and Order Document *Baptism, Eucharist and Ministry* urges:

> 'In order to overcome their differences, believer baptists and those who practise infant baptism should reconsider certain aspects of their practices. The first may seek to express more visibly the fact that children are placed under the protection of God's grace. The latter must guard themselves against the practice of apparently indiscriminate baptism and take more seriously their responsibility for the nurture of baptized children to mature commitment to Christ.'

World Council of Churches, *Baptism, Eucharist and Ministry*, Faith and Order Paper No. 111, copyright © 1982 World Council of Churches, ISBN 2-8254-0709-7, 30th printing, 1996. Para B16

In large parishes where there is a team of people taking bookings it is essential that they all work to the same policy and guidelines. It helps if neighbouring churches understand each other too, even if they don't operate identically. It is often useful for a deanery to produce a regularly updated document which sets out the policy and practice of each church, and gives the appropriate contact details, so that those who approach the 'wrong' parish can be helpfully directed straight to the people who can help in their local church.

Treating baptism as a sacrament with real significance, though, does not mean presenting an assault course to enquirers – sometimes with live hostile fire. Remember that the task is to urge people to deepen their faith, not intimidate them or convince them to leave it behind. They wouldn't be contacting us in the first place if they weren't responding to some religious urge, even a second-hand one.

Laura's story is probably not unfamiliar to many people who are regularly in receipt of baptism requests. This suggests that there may be a number of very predictable pressure points. There is no reason why these shouldn't have been thought through by local churches so that the response is understood and supported by a broad base of people.

Adopting a hospitable approach

The congregation, the church volunteers, staff and the enquirers all need to know where the boundaries are. Some of the points listed below may seem obvious, but clarity on each one is essential. They are taken in the order they were raised by 's story:

The age of the candidate

There is no minimum age for baptism but it may not be wise on pastoral grounds to take a booking before a baby is born (as is occasionally requested) as there are many grounds for uncertainties.

See sections C2 in relation to older children and C1 in relation to adults.

The relevant Canons are included in the Appendix, beginning on page 209 below.

An unknown or undisclosed parent

The Canons of the Church of England are silent about this issue, but churches have no legal grounds either for denying a baptism or for insisting on the information. Sometimes, however, a sensitive enquiry about whether dad (or mum) is 'around' can help the church not to make assumptions either way, and can prevent later *faux pas*.

Canon B 22.4 gives the minister the right to delay baptisms for instruction to take place. Beware that unduly long delays can be counter-productive and lead to appeals to the Bishop. (Canon B 22.2)

The faith of the parents

The Canons of the Church of England expect that the minister of baptism will offer instruction to the parents. ➤ This is where the local church can make a deep and positive impact.

➤**C4**

Parish of residence

If the child does not live in the parish (and neither of the parents is on the electoral roll) the goodwill of their own parish minister must be sought (though not necessarily obtained) before the baptism takes place (Canon B 22.5).➤

➤**B5**

Signposting

Many churches are extraordinarily weak in signposting to people how they should go about getting in touch or making enquiries. Clear phone numbers, office hours (even for the vicarage) and proper signage for buildings and their entrances are all essential.

Access

Parents with young children tend to have buggies, prams or bulky car seats. Easy access and buggy storage needs to be considered. Ensure the environment is child-friendly and consider having a few toys available. The alternative, of course, is to take some basic details and arrange to visit the parents in their own home at a time that is convenient to them and fits around their child's routine.

Confidentiality

Many people do not like to give out personal information in open public places, or to overhear others doing so. Make sure there is good differentiation between waiting areas and interview space. This helps give confidence that you will treat the information you are given responsibly.

Sticking to the 'rules'

The seasoned jobsworth can receive every enquirer as a potential problem. It is possible to offer a warm and open approach while still applying clarity and rigour when a request isn't straightforward. Choose volunteers carefully and have agreed responses for when people refuse either preparation or instruction (in practice most unlikely).

Language

If you use a term like 'vestry hour' or 'surgery' for the time when people come to make christening bookings, you may cause confusion or concern. There may be more straightforward labels, such as 'Open Evening' or 'Enquiry Hour'.

Watch the words you use. Words such as 'baptism', 'initiation', 'worship', 'confirmation', 'font', 'preparation', 'parish' and 'surgery' are jargon and likely to be misunderstood by some people if used without interpretation.

A number of the issues that are faced by people making their first contact with the church to arrange a baptism can be constructively handled by creative use of a web site. Consider making information about the services you offer, and your application forms for baptism and Thanksgiving for the Gift of a Child available as a download with clear notes to help people complete them. In a society that increasingly does business via the internet, the first hit on a web site might be a much easier place to start than knocking on a door or making a phone call.

Questions for discussion

1. How many contacts might an applicant have to make with the church before being able to book a service?

2. How child-friendly are our times and venues for making enquiries?

3. How might our system seem if we looked at it with a stranger's eyes?

4. What is the difference in meaning and nuance between 'Christening', 'Getting the baby done' and 'Baptism'?

Developing a parish policy

All parishes will need some sort of policy to define how initiation will be handled. Without a thought-through approach, practice will develop by accident, often dependent on the preferences of a series of incumbents. This may work, but it will not necessarily be the best pattern possible. Parishes are generally better at working out policies for baptism than for confirmation. This is largely because requests for infant baptism often present pressing practical issues (for instance, 'How can we fit them all in?').

In this section we look at some of the issues to be considered when putting a policy together, give some examples, and look at ways of making sure that the policy includes a look at the wider initiation questions, not simply infant baptism.

The text below comes from the commentary in *CW Christian Initiation* (page 318).

Parish policies on initiation

'Parishes and congregations need to have a clear and developing grasp of their approach to Christian initiation. This implies the involvement of the PCC (or equivalent) and wider church fellowship, not simply an initiative by the clergy. What is more, such parish policies and approaches must have regard for those particular concerns which are embodied in the bishop's oversight of initiation. This means that each parish would need to identify and own its approach to the welcome and formation of new believers. These approaches should be worked out in appropriate dialogue with the bishop and should cover:

¶ the welcome, formation and sacramental initiation of adult enquirers

¶ an appropriate pattern for responding to requests by non-churchgoing parents for their children's baptism

¶ an appropriate pattern for the admission to communion of baptized children

¶ provision (where appropriate) marking the entry into adulthood of young people growing up within the Church.'

Bishops may delegate this task to members of their staff more closely involved with the mission of the individual church.

[See also *On the Way*, pages 89 and 110-11]

Why and how: the process

Church members may well live in the same street as those applying for baptism for their children. Ideally, they should be able to explain the policy over the back fence to their neighbours. And their attitudes will vary from those who would never baptize a young child to those who think that no qualifications at all are needed for infant baptism. The corporate nature of baptism demands that a policy is formed, owned and supported by the church as whole. Those responsible for the policy will need to

- give plenty of time for as wide a range of people as possible to understand the underlying issues and complexity which the resulting policy will reflect;
- organize a conference, study day (perhaps away from the parish), teaching sermons, discussion material and written reports;
- manage the involvement of the bishop or his representative;
- ensure the Church Council owns the policy and sets a date to review it, evaluating it against the current mission criteria of the church;
- take account of Canon Law and any diocesan guidelines.

Baptism policy

Historically, a baptism policy in a Church of England parish has usually meant a policy about how *infant* baptisms are handled. However, as infant baptisms decline in number, and adult baptisms (or the baptism of older children) become more common, policies need to look at the wider picture.

Infant baptism

The number of 'christening enquiries' from parents who are not regular members of the congregation will vary from parish to parish and from one part of the country to another. In some places it has become minimal, but in many other parts of the church, this is still **A2** the dominant factor in initiation policies.

Where there is a significant number of enquiries, there will often be conflicting views among clergy and church members as to how those enquiries should be responded to. There are often obvious dilemmas: everyone wants to welcome visitors, but not everyone wants them to dominate Sunday services week after week. Some feel frustrated or 'used' by those who only come to church for christenings; others see the potential for making contacts that may bear fruit later.

Practical factors often play a much larger part in determining a policy for infant baptism than they do in determining patterns of adult baptism or confirmation.

The Canons encourage us to make baptisms part of a main service, but if the church building is small, and the number of enquiries is large, then questions soon arise. Not surprisingly, many churches find that despite their best intentions, a 'private' (or semi-private) service is the only realistic option. A policy then has to consider how to welcome the newly baptized into the family of the Church.

It will be wise, in these circumstances, for clergy and the church council to put in place a policy of some kind that will spell out how the parish will respond to requests, what options will be offered, and how the best possible use can be made of the opportunity that such contact brings. Because of the variety of situations, no 'one-size-fits-all' policy will be appropriate. Rather, the policy will be determined both by theological understandings of baptism and by local factors.

Factors affecting the development of a local policy will include things such as:

- the type and culture of the neighbourhood;
- the size and tradition of the church;
- the expectations of church members; and
- the expectations of the local community.

So, before we look at some sample policies, we begin by considering some of the issues which often arise during the discussion of any policy.

Common issues

Believing and belonging

The New Testament background gives examples of those who come to faith and are baptized without any preparation, and of whole families apparently spontaneously coming to baptism. Alongside this is the call to repentance and faith, and baptism as a sign of this new start. ☛ The policy which a church develops will reflect the understanding of this relationship between belonging and believing.

➼ A4, A5

In some parts of the Church, the focus is on baptism as the *starting point* of a person's life in Christ and the beginning of their discipleship, albeit with an undeveloped and tentative faith. Baptism signals belonging, which is seen as coming before, and leading to, believing. The sense of belonging may be linked to family and community more than to faith, and confusion over where baptism fits in makes for difficult pastoral dilemmas.

> 'It is desirable that every minister … shall normally administer the sacrament of Holy Baptism on Sundays at public worship when the most number of people come together, that the congregation there present may witness the receiving of them that be newly baptized into Christ's Church, and be put in remembrance of their own profession made to God in their baptism.'
>
> Canon B 21

In other parts of the Church, the focus is on baptism *as a milestone on the journey*, recognizing that a definite and committed decision has been made, based on a more developed understanding of the faith. Believing is seen as the gateway to belonging. The danger is that baptism becomes seen as a reward, withheld until a certain level of faith is attained.

The particular balance between these views (and any number of variations on them) will affect, for instance, the amount and type of preparation offered before baptism takes place.

When the candidate is an infant, this is further affected by the degree and expression of faith of the parents and godparents.

Welcoming and discerning

Behind the *Common Worship* initiation services there is a renewed emphasis on journey and story. To echo this, the policy will need to have a sense of progression, taking a person or family further along their personal faith journey within the context of the wider church. It should therefore look to all aspects of welcome and nurture, not just preparation for the service itself.

It is in this context of journey that the decision as to whether a candidate or their family is ready needs to be addressed. Too many hurdles can stifle a young or tentative faith, and too few can lead to what some have termed 'liturgical lying' - allowing people to go through the motions without a sense of the significance of what they are doing or saying. Integrity for the minister, church and participants will mean facing this issue as a church. If the request is made with integrity and the level of faith is honestly expressed - even if minimal - then the service will have integrity too. Openness to the welcoming and compassionate Spirit of Christ is needed alongside a solid commitment to the importance of baptism to the church.

Nurturing faith

Building steps and stages into the pre-baptism process will help to foster and develop the faith of the applicant and make the decisions above easier. A policy that seeks to move people forward, rather than seeing it as a pass or fail assessment, is clearly one to be encouraged. Developing the right policy for a parish will therefore include identifying what steps would be appropriate in a particular situation to ensure this.

The post-baptism programme of teaching and faith development may also need addressing, depending on the level of church provision already in place.

Parental faith and life

The parents play the key part (alongside godparents) in bringing up children to grow into the faith professed on their behalf at baptism. ➤ If the parents do not have faith themselves, then this is an area of pastoral concern and needs attention. It is increasingly common to meet parents who have not been confirmed and, occasionally, those where neither has been baptized either. This can be addressed by the whole family preparing for a service ➤ at which both baptism and confirmation are administered, so that each family member makes their profession.

➤B7

➤C2

Where one of the parents has no faith, or professes a different faith, there is no bar to baptism as long as *one* parent can take on the faith responsibility alongside the godparents. There is again a pastoral need to work through with parents how they are intending to make sure the children can be brought up within the Christian faith if the parents are themselves divided over the issue.

A baptism request can also act as a catalyst for assessing different aspects of family life. For some parents this may include marrying, if not already married, and reviewing lifestyle and values. A baptism policy which provides opportunity for faith development of the parents and godparents is therefore helpful.

Baptism and Thanksgiving

The provision of the two services, Thanksgiving for the Gift of a Child ➤ and Holy Baptism, has itself been a factor in forming policies in some parishes.

➤B4

Parents are often clear that they want to bring the child to church, to receive God's blessing, and to know that they have done the best they can for their child. They are sometimes less clear that they want to commit their child to membership of the Christian Church. It is these cases, rather than the clearer ones where faith and commitment to the Church is strong, that underlie the difficulty in forming parish policies. The Thanksgiving service can be a good first step for such parents, offering the assurance of God's love without the commitment of baptism, and many parishes now include the option of a thanksgiving as an important way of helping parents to discern what they are really seeking from God.

Forming a policy

Three key elements

A baptism policy will include a whole range of issues and practicalities, but they fall into three basic areas:

What happens before a baptism takes place?

B1➤
- How will the initial enquiry be dealt with? ➤
- Who will be the first contact?
- What options will be given?
- What literature or other resources will be used?

C1 - C4➤
- What preparation will there be for the candidate (or, if the candidate is an infant, for the parents and godparents)? ➤

C2➤
- What liturgical material will be used in the process of preparing for baptism? ➤

C3➤
- For an infant, what flexibility will be applied to non-confirmed godparents? ➤
- What is the likely timescale between first enquiry and actual baptism?

B6➤
- How will applications for baptism from outside the parish be handled? ➤

In what context will baptism be administered?

B5➤
- Will baptisms normally take place in a main Sunday service? ➤
- Will adults be baptized in a 'normal' service? Or will they be encouraged to be baptized and confirmed in the same service, either when the bishop comes, or at a cathedral Confirmation service?
- Will baptisms take place in a Eucharist, or only during all-age or other non-eucharistic services?
- Will there be a regular pattern (for example, baptisms every fourth Sunday of the month) or a more flexible approach?
- What is the maximum number of candidates (or families) in any one service?
- Will there be the option of a private afternoon service?
- If so, what provision will there be for welcoming the child to the congregation?

What will follow baptism?

- Will adults be encouraged to join home groups or other nurture groups? ➤   ➤**E2**
- For infants, how will parents be kept aware of church news and provision for children and their families? ➤   ➤**E1**
- Will there be any specific opportunity to reflect on baptism – perhaps a discussion opportunity for adults, or some sort of annual celebration of baptism for those whose children have been baptized in recent years? ➤   ➤**E3**
- How does admission to Holy Communion fit into a child's growth in faith? ➤   ➤**B8**
- How and when will adult candidates for baptism be encouraged to be confirmed as well? ➤   ➤**A6**
- How will the church encourage older children and teenagers to consider confirmation? ➤   ➤**B3**

Canon law

Baptism is a gift from God administered by the Church. It is for the Church to decide whether baptism is appropriate and when the time is ripe. The rules are intended to hold together the integrity of the commitment of baptism and its relation to mission and pastoral care. Baptism may, therefore, be delayed for the purposes of preparation. In case of undue delay, or refusal, on the part of the *local* church, recourse can be made to the bishop, whose decision is final. Working out the means of adequate and realistic preparation of candidates and/or their families will therefore be part of the policy. Dioceses will often have a policy statement related to baptism which reflects Canon law and adds its own further requirements.

Canon law – Canon B 22

2. If the minister shall refuse or unduly delay to baptize any such infant, the parents or guardians may apply to the bishop of the diocese, who shall, after consultation with the minister, give such directions as he thinks fit.

4. No minister shall refuse or, save for the purpose of preparing or instructing the parents or guardians or godparents, delay to baptize any infant within his cure that is brought to the church to be baptized, provided that due notice has been given and the provisions relating to godparents in these Canons are observed.

Canon B 22: Of the baptism of infants

Four sample infant baptism policies

1. Step by step

A policy based on the process of building church connections, using both thanksgiving and baptism and with thorough follow-up.

Key aspects

- When the enquiry is received a leaflet is sent which explains that the Thanksgiving service is a first step for all families.
- Enquiries are positively encouraged, and the church often makes the first approach to parents via contacts made through primary school, toddler group or post-natal groups.
- All parents are visited by the minister and a young parent. The Thanksgiving service is explained and a date booked.
- Thanksgivings take place during any convenient main Sunday service, and parents are encouraged to come to church to see one before theirs takes place.
- The Thanksgiving service is followed by a second visit, at which baptism is discussed.
- Baptism preparation follows, consisting of two Saturday morning sessions involving lay leaders, with a crèche provided. Parents are encouraged to come to see a baptism before the baptism of their own child.
- Baptisms are always in a main Sunday morning service.
- After the baptism, a follow-up visit is made by a lay member of the baptism preparation team.
- A second follow-up visit is made, either by the same person, or by an allocated 'baptism Aunt' (or 'Uncle'), who continues to make contact with anniversary cards.
- A weekly service for pre-school-age children (and accompanying adults) builds the friendships and covers the years before Sunday school, enabling continuing contact with the family.
- A service is held once a year for all those baptized, with photographs of the children mounted in a display at back of church.

Factors that shaped this policy

- A mobile community in a new housing area with a church building only 30 years old and little sense of continuity of contact with the church from generation to generation.
- Desire to draw people into a thriving and welcoming fellowship.

- A large number of young families means that the first contact is often made in the pre-natal and maternity units with congregation families.
- A mobile population means that contacts have to be encouraged without delay to maximize the months they are in the parish.
- Offering thanksgiving as a first step gives all families an initial welcome and is enough for some, enabling them to say 'no' to baptism with integrity if they feel unable to make the commitment involved. Others go on to baptism for their child, and some to confirmation preparation for themselves.
- The process uses lay involvement considerably – but without clergy abdication!

2. Belong and believe

A policy based on fellowship and incorporation, which encourages parents to take the commitment of baptism seriously.

Key aspects

- The enquiry is followed up by a visit by the clergy, at which the preparation process is explained and initial questions answered.
- For baptism preparation, parents are encouraged to join the Alpha course, which is run by lay people.
- Godparents who live nearby are also sent invitations to the Alpha course.
- Part-way through the course a provisional date is booked for a baptism service.
- Parents are encouraged to come along to church while they are on the Alpha course.
- At the end of the course, two of the lay leaders visit the parents to discuss their reaction to the course and whether they wish to proceed with the baptism, or consider the option of a Thanksgiving service.
- The Baptism service date is confirmed, or a Thanksgiving service may be booked instead.
- If a baptism is chosen, it takes place in a main service, usually on the first Sunday in the month, which is the all-age service. There may be more than one child being baptized.
- Follow-up invitations are given to the parents in the months following the service, to nurture courses, special events at church, and activities for children, such as the monthly Saturday morning children's service.
- Anniversary cards are delivered in person for the first three years by the lay leaders of the Alpha course.

Factors that shaped this policy

- A desire to help parents to explore their own faith as they prepare for the baptism of their child.
- A congregation who felt that many families had abused the more open policy operated during the time of the previous incumbent.
- A desire by the church council that infant baptism be administered with as much integrity as possible.

3. 'You are part of the story'

A policy based on a culture of belonging, and on building relationships for long-term mission.

Key aspects

- An initial brief visit is made by clergy to welcome the family's approach and make contact.
- A second, main visit is made by a lay baptism visitor to discuss details of future baptism arrangements. Informal teaching on the meaning of baptism and the gospel is given in this one-to-one context and printed resources are left for further reflection.
- Contact with the weekly parent and toddler group (or equivalent) is encouraged, and a further visit is made to finalize baptism details, discuss the resources which were left, and to encourage continuing exploration.
- The Baptism service takes place, usually at 12 noon on a Sunday, after the main morning service. The lay baptism visitor and a few others try to be present to represent the wider congregation.
- The welcome and the presentation of the baptism certificate is done as part of the main monthly family communion on a date following the baptism. This offers another opportunity to encourage regular attendance and involvement in church life.
- If the family is not resident in the parish, sometimes the welcome and presentation of the certificate is done in the 'home' parish, in liaison with the clergy there.
- Lay baptism visitors build a continuing relationship where possible and attend the baptism and the welcome, in a prominent role.
- An annual card is given on the anniversary of the baptism, with a renewed invitation to a parent and toddler group (or similar), family services, and other child-friendly events and activities.

Factors that shaped this policy

- This is a geographical area, a rural community perhaps, in which the connection with church is very strong, related to place and to family history across the generations.
- With strong local and family expectation, the response to enquiries can make or break a continuing pastoral relationship, and either further or frustrate the mission to the whole community.
- The child may not be resident in the parish, as the parents have left the area for work or more affordable housing, even though they feel strongly that their roots are still in the parish. This requires coordination with 'home' parish clergy, and consideration of issues relating to preparation and follow-up.
- The church building is small, only seating a hundred, and the regular congregation is around thirty, so if there are eighty visitors for baptisms the church is just too small.
- The church has decided to make the best of it, and sees a separate service as the opportunity for specific and focused communication of the gospel with that one particular family and their contacts.
- Lay participation in the process is patchy due to small numbers of potential helpers.
- Courses and regular teaching don't fit easily in this community.

4. 'The choice is yours'

A policy which offers an either/or approach to thanksgiving and baptism.

Key aspects

- When an enquiry is received, details are taken and a leaflet is sent straight away, which explains that there is a choice of service: thanksgiving or baptism. Thanksgivings are offered either in a main service, or as a private service at a date and time to suit the family. Baptisms are always in a main Sunday service.
- A week later, the vicar rings to arrange to visit the family. The difference between the two kinds of service is explained, questions are answered and application forms for both services are left.
- If the thanksgiving application is returned, the date is booked (to suit the parents if at all possible) and the service takes place without further preparation.

- If the baptism application is returned, a date is booked (to fit with the needs of the parents *and* the church) and preparation is organized.
- Baptism preparation consists of a visit from a lay baptism visitor. A short video is shown, questions are answered, and the visitor talks through the Baptism service, explaining both its meaning and the practicalities of where to stand and what you have to say.
- Parents are encouraged to come to church before the baptism takes place.
- Anniversary cards are sent for thanksgivings and baptisms, but only for the first two years.

Factors that shaped this policy

- A desire to give people genuine choices to help them to think about what they are hoping for from God.
- A large number of enquiries every year, which previously meant that some baptisms needed to take place outside main services. Since the option for a thanksgiving as a private service was introduced, the numbers of baptisms have become more manageable and they are now easily accommodated in main Sunday services.
- A shortage of lay people with time to get involved in the process. The reduced numbers of baptisms means that the lay visitors can cope.
- Positive feedback from parents bringing a second or third child about the relief they felt in being offered a choice, rather than baptism being the only option (as had been the case previously).

Confirmation policy

Because the practical issues are not so pressing and the numbers not (usually) so great, many parishes do not have any sort of thought-out confirmation policy, but simply an inherited pattern which gets adjusted as the years go by.

The different views and ways of handling confirmation in a mission setting ➤ will lead to different practical policies. Some of the issues discussed might be:

➤ A6

- Is confirmation mainly about admission to communion? Or is it chiefly an opportunity for Christian education? Is it seen as a time for the candidates to proclaim that the faith is real to them personally?
- Another possibility discussed in *Rites on the Way* is whether the church is using confirmation to mark the human transition from childhood to adulthood. This might be 'an annual event in its own right, not necessarily associated with the baptism, confirmation or reaffirmation of people of other ages ... [with] appropriate social activities to express its meaning for young people and the parish'.

[*Rites on the Way*, page 92]

- What is the place of the Confirmation service in the church's mission strategy? What, for instance, are the expectations about the use of testimonies?➤

➤ D6

- What about the role of the bishop in initiation: is it limited to confirmation?

'... each parish would need to identify and own its approach to the welcome and formation of new believers. These approaches should be worked out in appropriate dialogue with the bishop.'

Commentary, *CWCI*, page 318

- How does the practice of admitting children to Holy Communion before confirmation – a practice which is growing in the Church of England, and looks set to continue to do so – impinge on confirmation policy? Even parishes which do not adopt this pattern will find it affects them when children move to the parish from another church which does admit children to communion.➤

➤ B8

Key elements

The key elements of any confirmation policy will be the same as those for a baptism policy, though obviously the outworking will be different.➤

➤ B2

What happens before confirmation

- What is the minimum age for confirmation in our church?
- Will we apply this rigorously or with flexibility, according to the maturity of the candidate?

- If we allow admission to Holy Communion before confirmation, how will this affect our practice? (For instance, will it affect the minimum age for confirmation? Will it affect the content of any preparation course?)
- Will young people and adults be prepared for confirmation together or separately? (This will be affected by questions about the minimum age for confirmation, and the size of the church or group of churches.)
- What material and resources will we use for preparation? Are there existing structures of outreach and nurture that should be part of the preparation package (for instance, a youth group, or Alpha or Emmaus courses)?
- How long should confirmation preparation last?

In what context will confirmation be administered?

- Do we have an annual Confirmation service in our benefice, team ministry, group of parishes or deanery?
- If there is a deanery or multi-church confirmation how do we overcome the problems of combining different cultures and different expectations of confirmation, for example if some candidates want anointing (or baptism by submersion) and **D12** ◄ others do not? ◄
- Will we encourage candidates to get confirmed at cathedral Confirmation services?
- What are the pros and cons of taking candidates to a major diocesan Confirmation in the cathedral?

Away from home?

Susie, vicar of St Nathaniel's, takes three 16-year-olds and two adults to a deanery combined baptism and confirmation on a Sunday evening at St Cyprian's. There are six different parishes plus the bishop himself with a stake in how the service is **D11** ◄ conducted. ◄ The host incumbent has been responsible for pulling the whole thing together and liaising with the bishop's office, but Susie has been sufficiently involved to feel that none of St Nathaniel's policies are being undermined.

On the night the weather is awful, which means a smaller turn-out than expected, but there is a good atmosphere, and the sound of the singing drowns out the howling of the wind around the turrets of St Cyprian's. As people gather, Susie compares the **D6** ◄ testimonies ◄ she has provided from her candidates in the service booklet with those from the other churches, which reflect different approaches to confirmation. One of her candidates is a local radio presenter and does a reading. Two of the others are interviewed about their personal stories and the bishop draws together different threads from the testimonies in his sermon.

The following Sunday morning the signed certificates are given to the candidates in the main service, after an eyewitness account of the service from one of the sponsors. 'When we got to St Cyprian's it was great to see the church full, and to realize that people were coming from all those other churches around and about. And the way those kids led the prayers – I'd love to see us do something like that at our church one day.' And one of the candidates says to Susie after the service 'Those interviews made my partner think – he's been asking me questions about Jesus ever since ...'

What will follow confirmation?

- Will adults be encouraged to join home groups or other nurture groups? ➤
- Is there regular provision for young people in our church?
- How are those recently confirmed encouraged to be part of other church activities, for example reading or leading intercessions, or the church's decision-making processes?

➤**E2**

B4 Thanksgiving for the Gift of a Child

Go back just over one hundred years, and you find Church of England churches offering not only baptism, but also the service of 'Churching'. Even today, older members of congregations sometimes remember (or remember stories from their mothers) about the perils and superstitions which surrounded not being properly 'churched' after childbirth. Friends and family would often refuse to have a new mother under their roof until she had been churched, for fear of bringing bad luck on the household.

What is 'Churching'

In *The Book of Common Prayer*, slipped in between *The Burial of the Dead* and *A Commination or Denouncing of God's Anger Against Sinners*, is the two-page service called *The Thanksgiving of Women after Child-birth, commonly called The Churching of Women.*

This service simply did what it said: thanks were offered to God for a safe delivery (childbirth being a peril for both mother and baby) and prayers were said for the mother. In popular understanding, though, the service was associated with the idea that childbirth made a woman unclean, and some sort of service was required to cleanse her so that she could once again participate in normal society.

Understandably, the twentieth century saw a rapid decline in the use of the service, as the idea of a mother being unclean was no longer accepted.

Giving thanks for a child

Though few would now look for a service to 'cleanse' a mother after childbirth, there is still a natural desire to say 'thank you' to God when a child is born, and to seek his blessing on that child. ◄

D1, D2 ►

The Alternative Service Book 1980 included a service of Thanksgiving for the Birth of a Child, and *Common Worship* has updated it further in the Thanksgiving for the Gift of a Child. The slight change of title reflects two important points:

- the service can work just as well for welcoming an *adopted* child into a family; and
- the service may be appropriate for older children as well as for newborn infants.

'Baptisms and Churchings at St Peter's Church on Wednesday evenings at 7, and the first Sunday afternoon in every month, at 2.15 and 3.45. At these times one of the Clergy always attends without notice. Baptisms and Churchings can also take place at or after any weekday morning service.'

A Parish Magazine, January 1887

'The Woman, at the usual time after her delivery, shall come into the Church decently apparelled, and there shall kneel down in some convenient place, as hath been accustomed, or as the Ordinary shall direct ...'

Rubric at the start of *The Book of Common Prayer* service of Churching

Meeting contemporary needs

The production of the *Common Worship* service was an opportunity to reflect on the experience of using the ASB service. Several changes resulted.

Blessing a child

The ASB service avoided all hint of a blessing of the child; the CW service explicitly includes one, recognizing that the idea of having a child 'blessed' is often the way that parents articulate their desire for God to 'do something' for their child.

The 'blessing' is phrased in such a way as to allow for a minister who is not a priest (such as a Reader or a deacon) to use it as printed:

> As Jesus took children in his arms and blessed them, so now we ask God's blessing on *N*.

> Heavenly Father, we praise you for *his/her* birth;
> surround *him/her* with your blessing
> that *he/she* may know your love,
> be protected from evil,
> and know your goodness all *his/her* days.

[*CWCI*, page 19]

Naming a child

In the popular mindset, 'christening' is closely connected with the idea of naming (we still say we 'christen' something when we use it for the first time, or give it its name). The CW service recognizes this cultural connection and makes something of the use of the child's name in the service:

> *The minister may say for each child*
> What name have you given this child?

> *A parent or supporting friend replies*
> *His/her* name is *N*.

[*CWCI*, page 19]

It isn't quite a 'naming', but it is a public use of the name, picking up on the Prayer Book Baptism service's 'name this child' (which is not part of the CW Baptism service).

Appointing supporting friends

The option to appoint supporting friends, who in the service pledge themselves to support child and parents in the years to come, has been a great help pastorally. When parents begin to think about a christening, the first thing they think of is who will be the

Where to find the Thanksgiving for the Gift of a Child

The service is printed in several places:

CW Christian Initiation (page 16ff.)

CW Pastoral Services (page 200ff.)

CW main volume (page 337ff.)

Separate card (published by Church House Publishing)

Like all the other *Common Worship* services, it is available on the Church of England web site and as part of the *Visual Liturgy* service planning software.

godparents. The lack of godparents in a thanksgiving could be a big disincentive to people who, on other grounds, might welcome the chance to have a thanksgiving.

In addition, parents sometimes choose godparents who do not 'qualify' (perhaps because they are not baptized), and it can be useful to have a service in which those people can be recognized and given their role. There are no qualifications for being a supporting friend, other than a commitment to 'be there' for the child and family in the years to come, and you can appoint as many as you wish – which is sometimes helpful if family politics comes into play!

Who is the service for?

The note to the Service of Thanksgiving suggests three types of people for whom the service might be appropriate. The case studies below reflect real situations (though the names have been changed) which illustrate the three different ways that the service can be used.

Parents who see this as a preliminary to baptism

When **Richard and Mary** rang St Andrew's to book a christening they were hoping that it could be arranged for their wedding anniversary, in a month's time. Baptisms at St Andrew's are always in the main Sunday service, and they couldn't offer a slot for another two months. The vicar offered Richard and Mary the option of a private Thanksgiving service on their anniversary date, which they gladly accepted, and the child was later baptized at a monthly all-age service.

Parents who do not wish their children to be baptized immediately

Sonia and David have recently joined All Saints', having moved to the area. Previously they worshipped in a Baptist church and still feel uncomfortable about infant baptism. They wish their new baby to have the chance of a believer's baptism when she is older. In their Baptist church, parents were offered a service of Infant Dedication, and they see the Church of England's Thanksgiving service (suitably adapted) as an opportunity to ask for God's blessing on their baby and to commit themselves to giving her a Christian upbringing.

Paula has also recently contacted the parish office at All Saints'. Her mother has been encouraging her to 'have the baby done', but she feels unsure about it. She was asked to be a godparent some years ago and was surprised to discover how much spiritual commitment there was in the Baptism service, for parents and godparents. When the baptism visitors mention the existence of the Thanksgiving service, she is delighted. She books a date for the service and decides to try coming to church for a year, just for the monthly all-age service at first, and then to think again about whether to arrange a baptism for her child.

Others, who do not ask for baptism

When **David** rang the vicar he asked if the church did a naming ceremony. He and his partner had been to a secular naming for his brother's baby at a town hall, and they were hoping for something similar for their new baby. Not knowing who else to phone, he decided to try the church. Angela, the vicar, had never had a request quite like that, but realized that the Thanksgiving service might be closer to what David was looking for than baptism, and when she talked through the differences David and his partner were clear that the thanksgiving would be just right. The service, in the couple's home, was a big hit with their neighbours and friends, and resulted in a couple of enquiries from other parents.

Stephen had a church upbringing, but his wife, **Helen**, is an atheist. They both felt that baptism would not be appropriate for their new baby (Helen was very keen that the child should be able to 'make up his own mind about religion when he's old enough'). However, Stephen wanted to do 'something', and Helen agreed that a thanksgiving was a compromise that she could live with, as it did not commit them, or their child, to any ongoing involvement in the church.

Often, these initial situations begin to look even more complex as people tell their stories. The Thanksgiving can form the basis for a pastoral response in these cases too. For example:

Stephanie and **Mike** have been together for about two years. Their daughter Alicia was born three months ago, and they approached the church to enquire about a christening and decided on a Thanksgiving service. Stephanie is divorced, and has two other children, Philippa (8) and Ryan (6) from her former marriage. Neither of these children had been christened, as her former husband was very antagonistic towards the church. The Thanksgiving service became an opportunity to welcome baby Alicia into the world and into her family, to pray for God's blessing on Philippa and Ryan, and to pray for the whole family as they learn

A flexible option

Because a Thanksgiving doesn't have to be in a main Sunday service, or even in church (the note suggests the possibility of a private celebration at church or home) there is a lot more flexibility for families. Sunday lunchtime at church may still prove popular, but a Saturday afternoon celebration in the family's back garden, with a barbecue to follow, is just as appropriate, and may make it a more attractive option for some families. In addition, Thanksgiving services can often be booked in at much shorter notice, because they don't have to fit into the church's pattern of Sunday services.

to live and love together. A week before the Thanksgiving service took place, Stephanie rang the vicar again. She had just discovered that she had never been christened herself as a child: could the service include a prayer of blessing for her too?

How does this service relate to baptism?

One of the advantages of having this service in the church's 'toolkit' is that it releases baptism from being both a birth-rite and the sacrament of welcome into the family of the church. Thanksgiving can be offered as a service for welcoming a child into the world and into his or her human family; baptism may or may not follow, and is the way of welcoming someone of any age into the spiritual family of the Church.

As the case studies above show, the Thanksgiving service can be either a clear step on the road towards baptism, or part of a definite decision (for now) *not* to seek baptism. The former possibility is reflected in the placing of the service in the *CW Christian Initiation* volume (where it takes its place as a part of the approach to baptism) *and* in the *CW Pastoral Services* volume (which reflects its use as an occasional office, like funerals and weddings).

In either case, it is important that the parents and the church are clear about what is taking place, and what is *not* taking place. A register of services of Thanksgiving must be kept, just as for baptisms, and a certificate must be given. The certificate is vital for the child's sake, so that in the future (when memories of what took place are hazy) it will be clear that he or she can still be a candidate for baptism.

The service of Thanksgiving for the Gift of a Child is not to be confused with the separate option in the Baptism service, to include a prayer of thanksgiving for the child at the beginning. (See *CWCI*, page 166.)

In addition to these administrative safeguards against confusion, the congregational prayer immediately following the prayer of blessing makes it explicit that this has not been a baptism, by praying that the child will one day 'come through faith and baptism to the fullness of your grace'.

Where and when should a Baptism service be held?

How does the congregation view a Sunday that has a Baptism service? Is it seen as an opportunity to be reminded of their own baptism, to welcome visitors and potential newcomers to the church, and to celebrate the beginning of a new spiritual life (and possibly a physical life as well)? Or do they see it as an interruption to their normal routine, and a time when they may find 'their' seats occupied by strangers?

Integrating a baptism into a Sunday morning service ► needs careful handling, and the way it is done will change from one instance to another. In some situations, when the candidate or family have strong church connections, it would be almost unthinkable for the context to be other than the normal Sunday morning service of Holy Communion. On other occasions the link with the church is, so far, more tenuous, and the usual pattern may need some adaptation.

►D3

Where and when?

Canon B 21 says that 'every minister ... shall normally administer the sacrament of Holy Baptism on Sundays at public worship when the most number of people come together'. This is clearly meant to rule out some types of baptism service:

- the 'quiet afternoon baptism';
- a baptism in the family's front room;
- the midweek private service.

The use of the word 'normally', however, does mean that on occasion there might be some space for manoeuvre, where pastoral circumstances point us in that direction.

However, even with an intention to fulfil the 'normal' expectation, it is not always obvious how to apply it in practice, and common sense has to come into play. Imagine a church with a number of services on Sundays and midweek. The one with the greatest attendance, numerically, is the 8 p.m. student service on a Sunday evening. On a Sunday morning there is a well-attended BCP said communion followed by a Eucharist during which there are children's groups (with roughly the same number of adults as at the earlier service). Once a month the second service is replaced by Morning Praise, but numbers go down because some of the leaders and families take

> 'The canonical expectation (Canon B 21) is that baptism takes place within the course of public worship on Sunday. Within that, there are many possibilities, and these services provide structures for baptism and associated celebrations ... to take place in various contexts.'
>
> Introduction, *CWCI*, page 5

one Sunday a month 'off' to visit relatives. Strict application of the figures would tell us that all baptisms should 'normally' happen during the Sunday evening student service, long after children are in bed and far too late to follow the baptism with a party. Pastoral common sense says that the most suitable service is likely to be monthly Morning Praise, even though 'the most number of people' are not met together then.

The questions are similar in other circumstances: the smaller church, part of a team ministry or multi-parish benefice, which does not have a regular service each week; the midweek after-school service attended by children and carers, or the church structured on cell groups where everyone only gathers together once a quarter for a big celebration.

Those involved in taking decisions about location will want to consider:

- What is the main service for the candidate and their family?
- How important is the building to them? Is it important to be in a more permanent building (perhaps the old parish church), or in the normal worship centre (which might be a school)?
- Is the local congregation more important to them than the building – in which case it doesn't matter where it takes place?

The point of stipulating that baptism should take place 'at public worship when the most number of people come together' is that there should be a congregation of church members. Church members promise to support and nurture the baptized person, who is joining the community of faith; the whole congregation joins together in professing that faith. Both parts of the service require a significant attendance by church members. It is the community that is important, not the building or the place.

And baptism as part of regular worship is important *for* the community – it gives everyone a regular opportunity to remember their baptism, give thanks for salvation and receive the challenge to be outward-looking and mission-focused.

'The structure of the service [of Holy Baptism] enables it to be used as a significant celebration on its own and there may be occasions where such a celebration of Holy Baptism forms a main Sunday act of worship.'

Note 2, *CWCI*, page 98

Celebrations of baptism

In some churches it may be possible (and appropriate) to draw several baptisms together into one service, which then becomes a service whose chief focus is baptism. Such services could become a regular part of the worship pattern (for example, on the four 'fifth Sundays' in the year). Many of the regular church congregation can be drawn into such a special service, which would meet the requirement that 'the most number of people' were there.

Fitting baptism into the usual service

The regular Sunday service during which baptism is most likely to take place will without doubt be a Eucharist, Morning Prayer or some other Service of the Word (such as an all-age service). Of course, for these occasions, there is no reason why Holy Baptism (with eucharistic provision) or Baptism apart from a Celebration of Holy Communion cannot be used in their straightforward form. They are both printed in full in *CW Christian Initiation* (see pages 60ff and 80ff respectively).

Alternatively, the basic structure for the service can be A Service of the Word, Morning Prayer or Holy Communion, with the baptismal material inserted appropriately. Guidance for this is provided in a set of instructions in *CW Christian Initiation*, but full services are not printed.

The version for use at a Service of the Word leaves plenty of scope for creative flexibility, and the use of *Visual Liturgy* may help in opening up those possibilities.

The essential core is a block of liturgy that immediately follows The Liturgy of the Word:

- Presentation of the Candidates (which can be used earlier, in the Gathering or Preparation section)
- The Decision
- Signing with the Cross
- Prayer over the Water
- Profession of Faith
- Baptism
- Commission
- The Welcome and Peace also follow, but not necessarily immediately. In a Eucharist the Intercessions may precede this.

Changes to Order One Holy Communion

In a regular *CW* Order One Holy Communion, the incorporation of baptism generates a number of other changes:

- an appropriate introduction to the service is required;
- the Prayers of Penitence are omitted in favour of the Decision;

The instructions for fitting baptism into other services can be found in *CW Christian Initiation* as follows:
Baptism within a service of Holy Communion (Order One and Order Two/BCP): pages 78–9
Baptism at a Service of the Word: page 96
Baptism at Morning or Evening Prayer: page 97

For guidance on how baptism fits into Order Two/BCP, see page 79.

- the Creed or Affirmation of Faith is omitted in favour of the Profession of Faith;
- intercessions as provided in *CW Christian Initiation* may replace what is normally provided;
- a lighted candle is presented at the conclusion and consideration must be given as to how this is best done (see Note 8, page 78).

Baptism and the Church seasons

D4 ➜ Specific seasonal material is provided for Epiphany and Trinity, ➜ Easter to Pentecost and All Saints to Advent to help make connections between the baptism rite and the Church's year. This considerably helps the integration of these services into the regular worshipping life of a church. Those who use seasonal colours are also likely to want to keep to the colour of the season, rather than use white every time. The provision for each season includes:

- a seasonal introduction
- a baptismal collect specific to the season
- readings and psalms
- Gospel acclamation
- Prayer over the Water
- Introduction to the Peace
- prayers of intercession
- post-communion collect
- blessing

Baptism and pastoral reality

Common Worship baptism is designed to be noticed whenever it is incorporated into another service - it can't be squeezed in unobtrusively! However, where pastoral needs suggests that the normative provision is too long or wordy, a number of **D3** ➜ considerations have been made. ➜ They include:

- short responsive forms of Prayer over the Water (page 177, with seasonal forms on pages 152, 153, 158 and 162)
- brief form of intercession (page 179)
- alternative Profession of Faith (page 178)
- alternative form of the Decision (page 168)

An alternative form of the Decision

Therefore I ask:

Do you turn to Christ?
I turn to Christ.

Do you repent of your sins?
I repent of my sins.

Do you renounce evil?
I renounce evil.

Baptism in new expressions of church

Sometimes a request for baptism will come from an individual or a family worshipping as part of a 'fresh expressions' congregation - meeting midweek in a school or a pub, sometimes because Sunday mornings (or the church building) are totally unsuitable for them. Here the questions about community and place are very pointed. For some, the baptism service can serve as an introduction to the church building, for example when an adult has come to faith through an Alpha group meeting in a pub, or a child is to be baptized from the congregation meeting in the local school. It might be possible to take the whole group or congregation to the church building that week.

Alternatively, this may be a time to take the church community to the pub (or swimming pool or beach!) for the baptism, to demonstrate the unity between the congregations.☛ **☛B10, D10**

Where new ways of 'being church' are being developed, it will be important that the 'new expression' is seen as complete in its own right. This includes its being a baptizing and Eucharistic community. For some this might mean a minimalist use of the liturgy. In many it will mean considerably 'riching it up'.

Sometimes a baptism will take place away from the candidate's usual service. ☛ Here there are opportunities for marking the occasion (before or after the event, or both) so that the baptism is clearly marked and celebrated at the usual service, even though it actually happens elsewhere.

☛ [Some of the issues raised in section B5 may be relevant here]

Before the baptism there might be a service of Thanksgiving for the Gift of a Child, ☛ or an interview with, or testimony by, an adult candidate. After the baptism the event could be marked by a Celebration after an Initiation Service outside the Parish (pages 182-3: this also includes the opportunity for testimony), by the presentation of the baptism card or gift, or by the use of either or both of the Welcome and the Giving of a Lighted Candle.

☛B4, D2

Similar arrangements might be used for candidates to be confirmed away from their usual place of worship, as confirmations are often deanery or cathedral occasions and a limited number of the normal congregation go along. The Celebration after an Initiation Service outside the Parish is expressly designed for this as well as for baptism.

B6 Requests from outside the parish

Boundaries aren't what they were

The relation of parish boundaries to the neighbourhood boundaries observed by people outside the Church has become increasingly tenuous, especially in many inner city areas and large towns. A large post-war housing estate is likely to be divided by two or three parish boundaries and yet thought of as a single neighbourhood by its residents. Add to this the dramatic increase in people's mobility, with adult children scattered across the country, and rapidly changing notions of 'home' – and the practicalities of arranging a family celebration in the 'home church' look pretty problematic.

Canon B 22.5

A minister who intends to baptize any infant whose parents are residing outside the boundaries of his cure, unless the names of such persons or of one of them be on the church electoral roll of the same, shall not proceed to the baptism without having sought the good will of the minister of the parish in which such parents reside.

Requests from neighbouring parishes

In inner cities, outer estates and other similar places there is often no vestige of logic left on the ground for historic parish boundaries. People will relate to a church for all sorts of reasons – and the fact that it happens to be the parish church for their house will not always be one of them. Maybe it is the church next to their supermarket; maybe they belonged to the parent and toddler group there; maybe their grandfather was buried there; or maybe they prefer the tradition or style of worship. In a rural context, within a benefice or deanery, it may well be the church seen as the prettiest that gets the bulk of the christening enquiries.

In these situations there is a good case for some very flexible and co-operative working between parishes in their initiation strategies. This might usefully be part of a wider sharing of information about how requests are handled in neighbouring parishes, patterns of baptism preparation and, indeed, the resources that are used.

Possible strategies

There can be little credible rationale for an obstructive approach to baptism requests, although it is one of a number of strategies available. Those strategies, working from the most parochially minded to the least, might include the following:

No agreement for baptisms across boundaries

This would mean refusing to baptize those who do not live in the parish, and refusing to give goodwill to those in the parish seeking baptism elsewhere. This may help ensure that all the baptisms in a parish don't leak to a neighbouring church, and so ensure some contact for the particular parish with local young families. However, it is unlikely to be understood by those outside the church, may be resented, and will certainly become counterproductive. Even where church councils regret that old notions of localness are breaking down, the tide is unlikely to be turned back by Canute-like behaviour. Canon law, of course, only says that goodwill should be *sought* – not necessarily obtained – so such a policy would not necessarily have the desired effect if it were not respected by the requesting parish.

Formal letters exchanged for each request

The advantage of this approach is that it is possible for all the churches in a neighbourhood to monitor what is happening to baptism requests from each other's parishes. These days, neighbouring churches can easily exchange information about enquirers by email, which can be quicker and feel less formal and bureaucratic. Where clergy deal with these matters of protocol and good practice themselves there is usually little problem. However, it can become a more negative experience for the enquirers if clergy shift the responsibility for obtaining goodwill onto the family involved. Setting up such hoops for them to jump through is not likely to provide the best basis for trustful and respectful relationships.

General agreement to be flexible

This is easy for both applicants and churches, but requires a high level of trust between parishes. If one church thinks another is being predatory this can easily break down. Don't forget that each time there is a change of leadership in a church, the agreement needs renewing.

Change the boundaries

Sometimes, when parish boundaries make little sense and cause frustration, the best (though not the simplest!) long-term solution is to change the boundaries. This is the most helpful solution for those outside the Church.

In all of these examples it is likely that preparation will be the responsibility of the baptizing parish. Follow-up and nurture may be too, though sometimes it will be more natural for the parish in which the family live to take this on if they are geographically nearer, and/or there is no intention on the part of the enquirers to make a long-term commitment to the church in which the baptism takes place.

Requests from further afield

Baptism requests from the other end of the country, and even the other side of the world, are not unusual as travel has become easier and cheaper and as workforces are expected to be more mobile. This presents a further set of considerations.

The reason for the request

An Australian family is unlikely to request a baptism in an English parish church just for the sake of it. Probably such requests will come either because of historic family connections (Mum was baptized here twenty-five years ago) or, more likely, because of practicalities when most of the family, including aged grandparents, live in the parish. While the first is very tenuous, the second of these reasons can feel more substantial, but there is no legal compulsion for either to be agreed to. Careful pastoral consideration must be given. Answers should be clear and reasoned. Consistency is important. Agreement for one family and refusal to another will lead to misunderstanding.

Goodwill of the home parish minister

This should always be sought, whether by phone, email, or in writing from the Anglican incumbent where the family lives. It may be that the home parish has never heard of the family – or it may be that a complex pastoral situation is revealed that needs delicate handling at both ends. The minister faced with the request to baptize may consider a lack of goodwill at the other end of the phone to be sufficient reason to turn down the request, or may agree to the request as the best way forward for all concerned. Obtaining the home incumbent's goodwill can be harder where families live abroad, but it is helpful to understand their home church situation.

Preparation

Where families live a considerable distance from the baptizing parish, preparation may be difficult unless this consists of a single conversation. It may well be best if this can be done by their home parish; it could help to build the relationship between the family and their local church.

Public acknowledgement at home

Whether or not preparation is possible in the family's home parish, it is good if there can be some acknowledgement there that the baptism has taken place. The presentation of the child at worship there either before or after the baptism can also help cement relationships between the family and the local church.

Questions for discussion

1. Does your parish have a policy for handling requests for baptism from outside the parish (or requests for parishioners to have a baptism elsewhere)? If so, does it need reviewing?

2. Is there ever a good reason to refuse to extend goodwill to a baptism taking place elsewhere?

3. In what ways could you build links with a family who chose to have a baptism in another parish?

Before a baptism elsewhere: material from the Welcome of Those Preparing for the Baptism of Children could be used: *CW Christian Initiation*, page 31f.

After a baptism elsewhere: a simple form of words that may be used subsequent to a baptism may be found on page 182 of *CW Christian Initiation*. Alternatively, the welcome from the Baptism service itself can be used with suitable explanation, perhaps accompanied by the presentation of the baptism certificate, sent from the baptizing church.

Godparents and sponsors

Why have godparents?

Early Christians had 'godparents' because the person to be baptized often came from a non-Christian family. There might have been no one at home to support and mentor new Christians as they embarked on their new life in Christ.

The Baptism service recognizes that today the situation may be very similar. Our society is no longer one that could be labelled 'Christian', and although *practically* the parents are likely to be the key people in helping a child to grow up within the church and the Christian faith, godparents can also have an important role. Indeed, there is no formal requirement that parents who bring a child to be baptized are themselves believers, although Canon B 22.3 says the minister is to instruct the parents 'that the same responsibilities rest on them as are in the service of Holy Baptism required of the godparents', and the questions to parents and godparents at the presentation of infant candidates presuppose a Christian faith. What parents actually promise is to *support* the *child's* Christian upbringing. This may well include seeing their own faith develop and become more articulate at the same time. At the Decision and the Profession of Faith they speak on behalf of the child, not on their own behalf.

It is all the more important, then, that at least some of the godparents should be practising Christians in order that there may be support and encouragement for learning the Christian Way.

Many parents open a savings account 'on behalf of' their child; and will commit even a young child to a school or sports club. See the section on proxy speaking and parental faith in the Commentary, *CWCI* pages 340f.

Many of the candidates for baptism in the early Church would have been adults, and today we would have called their supporters 'sponsors'.

Godparents and sponsors

The roles of godparent and sponsor have much in common. At the heart of both is a commitment to support a candidate in the journey of faith. They are, however, distinct roles and there is often confusion surrounding them. Here's a quick guide to the differences.

Godparents

- Godparents are appointed at a baptism, and are only appointed if the candidate is an infant or child. Part of their role is to speak on behalf of the child, which is not required for adult candidates.
- Godparents have a dual role: spiritual *and* social. The social aspect is reflected in the expectations in popular culture of a godparent.

Sponsors

- Adults who are baptized have sponsors, rather than godparents, but infants and children can have sponsors at their baptism too.
- For a child or infant, sponsors are appointed *in addition to* godparents.
- A sponsor has a primarily spiritual role. (In the case of an infant or child, a sponsor might be ready to encourage the candidate in spiritual matters, but not feel able to make the commitment to more practical or social support, which the godparent role includes.)
- Confirmation candidates can also appoint sponsors. These are sometimes, but not always, the godparents and/or sponsors from their baptism.
- Sponsors may also be appropriate for those affirming their baptismal faith or being received into the Church of England.
- For adult baptism, confirmation, affirmation and reception, a sponsor's role is to 'vouch' for the candidate, and in the service it may include presenting them to the congregation and standing with them.

When the candidate for baptism is a child who can speak for him or herself, the boundaries become blurred, and much will depend on the age and maturity of the child and the views of the parents. Sometimes godparents will seem to be the best form of support; sometimes sponsors may seem more appropriate. At the Decision, the parents and godparents may speak for the child, or the child may answer with them, or the child may make his or her own promises.

For more information see Canon B 23 and *CW Christian Initiation*, page 99 (Note 6 to the service of Holy Baptism) and page 342 (the Commentary section).

How should godparents be chosen?

Some might think that parents would not begin to think about the choice of godparents until they have approached the church about the possibility of arranging a baptism. But in reality family members and friends may have been expecting to be asked to be a godparent for many months – may even have been promised the role by the child's parents.

The Church's image of godparents and the image in the mind of the new parent may be miles apart. Canon law (Canon B 24) has a very clear idea about the number and type of people who are suitable to be godparents. Many new parents, however, do not know anyone who goes regularly to church, and would struggle to find qualified friends or members of the family.

Canon B 23 Of godparents and sponsors

1. For every child to be baptized there shall be not fewer than three godparents, of whom at least two shall be of the same sex as the child and of whom at least one shall be of the opposite sex; save that, when three cannot conveniently be had, one godfather and godmother shall suffice. Parents may be godparents for their own children provided that the child have at least one other godparent.

2. The godparents shall be persons who will faithfully fulfil their responsibilities both by their care for the children committed to their charge and by the example of their own godly living.

3. When one who is of riper years is to be baptized he shall choose three, or at least two, to be his sponsors, who shall be ready to present him at the font and afterwards put him in mind of his Christian profession and duties.

4. No person shall be admitted to be a sponsor or godparent who has not been baptized and confirmed. Nevertheless the minister shall have power to dispense with the requirement of confirmation in any case in which in his judgement need so requires.

There is often a real tension between being as welcoming as we can to the enquiry, while trying to encourage a choice of godparents who recognize that the role is not merely honorary or social, and who are ready for a long-term, serious and spiritual undertaking. It is not easy for parents to withdraw an invitation to a relative or friend who, it turns out, will not be the right person. In situations where parents themselves, coming to understand the role of a godparent more fully, feel that they are caught in a dilemma, the service of Thanksgiving for the Gift of a Child ➤ can be a useful pastoral option. Parents can use a Thanksgiving service to appoint supporting friends from among those who will support them and their child more generally, and then plan a baptism for which they can chose a smaller number of godparents who will be comfortable with the spiritual role required.

➤B4, D2

Whom to choose?

These are some of the issues that might be relevant.

How many should there be?

- There should normally be at least three godparents, of whom two are the same sex as the child, and one is the opposite sex.
- The minimum number is one, if the mother and father stand as the other two godparents. This might make it easier if the parents are struggling to find baptized and confirmed godparents, but it also reduces to one the number of people outside the family looking after the spiritual development of the child.

There is no maximum number of godparents. 'At least three' means that it is perfectly in order to have more godparents than three, and some people do. (But an adult may choose a maximum of three sponsors - see page 74 below.)

While Kate was small we were living abroad, though we knew we would come back to England later. We opted to have two godparents from each country.

Who should they be?

Given that being a godparent is a serious spiritual commitment, what sort of people make the best godparents?

Members of the family have the advantage that they are less likely to lose touch, even if they live many miles away, and they will already have a relationship with the child. However, distance may make it harder for them to take a very active role.

Friends from work or neighbourhood, or from the past, add to the circle of people who care for the child, but may lose touch if they move away. Of course, this new responsibility may of itself cement and prolong the relationship.

Some churches offer to find a godparent from among the congregation - maybe a neighbour, another parent from the toddler group, someone involved in baptism preparation, or someone older

Godparents who are not confirmed

One way to combine flexibility with integrity (for both church and godparents) is to ask unconfirmed godparents to sign a simple declaration that they are Christians, that they believe and trust in Father, Son and Holy Spirit, and that they understand the spiritual role that they will be taking on as godparents.

It will not normally be pastorally helpful to 'police' this too tightly, but this is one way of making godparents aware that the church takes seriously their spiritual role, and of encouraging them to do likewise. It could be accompanied by some literature about baptism, encouragement to be part of any baptism preparation organized for parents, and perhaps the invitation to see their new role as a chance to explore their own faith, perhaps by attending a nurture course or enquirers' group.

Godparents and guardianship

Godparents are not necessarily the legal guardians to the child if both parents were to die, though sometimes parents ask a godparent if they are willing to be named in their wills as guardian.

whose own children have left home. This may help both the family and the church to keep the promise to stay in touch. It also means that at least one of the godparents will have a clear understanding of the spiritual role involved.

Restrictions

There is no minimum age for godparents, though the requirement that they should be confirmed implies that they should be over the usual confirmation age.

Canon law (B 23.4, see page 70) says that godparents must be baptized and confirmed. The intention here is to ensure that godparents are practising members of a church, who have publicly affirmed their Christian faith as adults. This makes a lot of sense if they are to be able to encourage their godchild to grow up within the church. In particular, a godparent should encourage the child to get confirmed when he or she is old enough. Obviously, that's hard to do if godparents are not themselves confirmed.

The minister does have discretion to dispense with the requirement of confirmation. This is designed for those cases where the godparent is from another Christian denomination, particularly one (such as the Baptist Church) which does not practice confirmation at all. It does, however, give some flexibility when parents are struggling to find anyone who is confirmed.

The commitment

The godparents, along with the parents, have to make promises at the start of the Baptism service which, at the very least, commit them to exploring Christian faith with the child as he or she grows up. After the minister has asked the whole church to welcome and support the baptized person, questions are put to the parents and godparents.

> Parents and godparents, the Church receives these children with joy. Today we are trusting God for their growth in faith. Will you pray for them, draw them by your example into the community of faith, and walk with them in the way of Christ?
>
> **With the help of God, we will.**
>
> In baptism these children begin their journey in faith. You speak for them today. Will you care for them, and help them to take their place within the life and worship of Christ's Church?
>
> **With the help of God, we will.**

The responsibility involves action, not just warm encouragement.

What should a godparent do?

There are plenty of things a godparent (or supporting friend at a Thanksgiving for the Gift of a Child) can do to support a child as he or she grows up, and they will vary with each child and each situation. It is sometimes harder to think about how to support a child *spiritually*.

Here are some ideas for the specific spiritual role of a godparent:

- pray;
- give gifts that encourage faith and exploration (such as Bibles, books, Christian computer software or DVDs and so on);
- be a good listener – especially to doubts or questions – and not too quick to give answers or close down conversation;
- keep in touch – letters, phone calls, emails, text messages – and let your godchild know that you are praying for him or her;
- encourage the child to experience Christian events beyond the local church (such as Taizé, Iona, or Spring Harvest) – or take them;
- encourage the child to experience Christian traditions other than that of their local church;
- encourage the child to get confirmed at an appropriate age – and maybe get involved in the confirmation preparation yourself, if that is feasible.

In some cases, thinking about the promises prompts someone who has been asked to be a godparent to consider confirmation for himself or herself. After all, if you are prepared to make the promises on someone else's behalf, why not make them for yourself?

What about godparents who can't be there?

Godparents should all be present at the baptism. One of their roles is to make promises, both on behalf of the child and for themselves. However, this is not always possible. Someone who is otherwise perfect for the role might be abroad or ill on the day. If this is the case, and the date really cannot be changed, it is possible for someone else to stand proxy for the godparent, and make the promises for them during the service. It's better to have the ideal person for the long term than to concentrate solely on availability for the service.

One way to help absentee godparents to feel 'part of things' is to send an explanatory leaflet and ask them to sign the declarations they would have made in the service itself.

Sponsors

Most of what has been said about godparents is equally applicable to sponsors. Ideally a sponsor is a mature Christian who can be a support, who can accompany the candidate through the preparation sessions, and afterwards be someone to turn to when there are questions. A sponsor, however, does not make promises on behalf of an adult: the essence of adult baptism, and of confirmation, is that the promises are made in person.

Two or three sponsors are usually chosen, but in some circumstances (particularly if the candidate is an adult and part of the church community) one may be sufficient. The choice may be natural - someone who has already been involved with the person to be baptized, maybe as part of an Alpha or Emmaus course, or a neighbour who attends the same church, or a trusted family

C3➤ friend. ➤ The person to be baptized or confirmed may already have ideas about who should be asked.

Questions for discussion

1. What guidance do you give to parents about how to choose godparents? Is there any way that this could be made clearer for them?

2. Are there any ways that you could involve godparents more actively in preparation for baptism, even if they live a long way from the church?

3. What guidance do you give to adult candidates for baptism, or candidates for confirmation, affirmation or reception, about choosing sponsors? Is there any way that this could be made clearer for them?

Admission to Holy Communion

It may appear that the traditional pattern for admission to Holy Communion in the Church of England is this: baptism as an infant, followed by confirmation in adolescence, which then allows you to receive Holy Communion. ➤ This pattern is in fact one developed (or at least reinforced) by reforming bishops in the Victorian era. *The Book of Common Prayer* includes another pattern: baptism in 'riper years', admission to Holy Communion because 'ready and desirous' of being confirmed, and confirmation soon after.

➤A6

Two approaches

In 1997 the House of Bishops issued new guidelines, which opened the door for there to be two parallel approaches to baptism, confirmation and communion within the Church of England. The first pattern was the 'inherited norm', linking the reception of Holy Communion to confirmation. But it also allowed another pattern to develop; baptism, admission to Holy Communion, and later confirmation.

The reasons given for allowing the alternative were various:

- Baptism is increasingly seen as complete sacramental initiation.
- Children, therefore, should not be excluded from the table, if they are included in God's people by baptism.
- The alternative pattern would ease the pressure for early confirmation, releasing it to be a rite of adult expression of faith.

Other questions were also being asked:

- Is the Church of England getting out of step with some provinces of the Anglican Communion, such as Canada and New Zealand, where all are admitted to Holy Communion on the basis of baptism?
- Is the Church of England also out of step with the Orthodox and Roman Catholic Churches?

The argument was not one-sided. For many in the Church of England, the existing pattern worked, and some feared that the alternative pattern would lead to a decline in confirmation. For others, the big issue is the question of understanding. If a certain (adult) level of understanding is required for admission to Holy

The second pattern in the Prayer Book was introduced in 1662 partly because of the 'growth of Anabaptism' and neglect of infant baptism during the Commonwealth period, partly to meet the needs of new Anglican missionary work overseas: 'may be always useful for the baptizing of ... others converted to the faith'.

(Preface to *The Book of Common Prayer.)*

'The Church needs to encourage awareness of many different levels of understanding, and support the inclusion of those with learning difficulties in the Christian community.'

Communion (which is the implication of linking it to confirmation), then the opening of communion to young children raises fears about 'irreverent' reception or inadequate understanding of the significance of the sacrament. This line of thinking, however, raises further issues for people with learning difficulties, who, on this argument, might never reach a required 'level' of understanding and be admitted to Holy Communion. The 1997 Guidelines recognized the importance of this as an issue for the Church.

The current situation

Dioceses developed various policies based on the 1997 Guidelines. After much experience and discussion, national regulations were agreed by General Synod in February 2006.

About 10 per cent of the parishes in the Church of England currently admit children to communion before confirmation.

Under the new regulations, the bishop of a diocese has to decide whether in principle to allow the admission of the baptized to communion before confirmation. Once the bishop has decided to allow the alternative pattern, any incumbent can apply to the bishop for specific permission for a particular parish.

The bishop will have to be assured that:

C4➤
- there has been thorough consultation among the congregation;
- the parish has made adequate provision for preparation;➤
- the parish has made provision for continuing nurture and encouraging children to come to confirmation in due time; and
- the church council has passed a resolution seeking approval to adopt the new pattern.

Once the bishop has given approval to the parish, it has to be remembered that:
- those admitted must be baptized;
- the parents must approve of admission;
- the admission to communion must be acknowledged in public

D9➤
   worship;➤
- a record of each child's name must be kept in a suitable register; and
- each child must also be given a record of their admission, either in the form of a certificate, or a note on their baptism certificate.

The existence of two parallel patterns has raised some practical questions, the most pressing of which is what to do if a child who has been admitted to communion in one parish then moves to another parish that still keeps to the traditional pattern. This is not new - it was already an issue when someone moved to a Church of

England church from a parish in a part of the Anglican Communion that admits children to communion. Now, however, the issue has become more local and a more common problem. Simply moving from one part of a deanery to another may raise the issue. The regulations, therefore, make clear that once someone has been admitted to communion in one parish, they cannot be refused communion in any other parish, even one in which the traditional pattern still holds.

> A child who presents evidence in the form stipulated in paragraph 9 that he or she has been admitted to Holy Communion under these Regulations shall be so admitted at any service of Holy Communion conducted according to the rites of the Church of England in any place, regardless of whether or not any permission under paragraph 4 is in force in that place or was in force in that place until revoked.
>
> Admission of Baptized Children to Holy Communion Regulations 2006

Questions for discussion

If your church currently operates the traditional pattern:

1. Do you think that the current pattern is working?

2. What are the aspects of the current pattern that are important for you?

3. How do the children in your church feel about waiting for confirmation before being admitted to communion?

4. What are the implications of your current pattern for the age at which confirmation takes place and the focus of confirmation – and are you happy with that?

If your church has moved to the alternative pattern:

1. Do you think that the new pattern is working? – and does *everyone* think so?

2. What are the aspects of the new pattern that are important for you?

3. Are there any families who have chosen for their children *not* to be admitted to Holy Communion? How do those children feel about the new pattern?

4. Are there any changes you need to make to the way you celebrate the Eucharist (or organize the children's work) to take account of the new pattern?

5. How can you make sure that children are still encouraged to come to confirmation – and at what age do you think this will now be most appropriate?

Reception from other denominations

The Church of England recognizes people who want to be received into its membership as having three different starting points (Canon B 28):

- Those who have not been baptized (or the validity of whose baptism can be held in question).
- Those who have been baptized but who have not been episcopally confirmed.
- Those who have been episcopally confirmed with unction or with the laying on of hands.

Of these three categories, the form of Reception into the Communion of the Church of England provided in *CW Christian Initiation* is designed primarily for the third.

[See D13 Affirmation and Reception for details of the services]

Those who are not baptized can be received simply by being baptized. Those who are baptized but not confirmed can be received by being confirmed (unless they are not yet ready for confirmation). The special form of Reception into the Church of England is, then, primarily for those who have already been episcopally confirmed, and who, therefore, cannot be confirmed again.

'If any such person has been episcopally confirmed with unction or with the laying on of hands he shall be instructed, and, with the permission of the bishop, received into the Church of England according to the Form of Reception approved by the General Synod, or with other appropriate prayers.'

Canon B 28.3

This part of the canon makes it clear that the form of reception provided in *CW Christian Initiation* is not the only form that may be used.

Respecting the past

In practice any candidate presenting for reception from another church is likely to have a mature faith and their desire to be welcomed into membership of the Church of England will be born out of a long experience of church, including some experience of the Church of England. Experience and growth in other church traditions needs to be respected for all candidates, whichever denomination they happen to come from. At no time should a candidate for reception from another Christian church be asked to reject their past. In addition, under no circumstances should there be any coercion.

Preparation

The preparation of candidates may depend on their previous denominational affiliation. This is much better judged on an individual basis than according to a prescribed approach for each denomination. Candidates who have drifted away from their previous church for some time before finding their way to the Church of England may find it helpful to prepare along with candidates for confirmation. For other candidates this may not be appropriate. Some will have already prepared themselves for this. Where the reception is to take place at the same time as baptisms, confirmations, and Affirmation of Baptismal Faith, it may be desirable for all the candidates to prepare together. Those of longstanding faith in other traditions may well be happy to do this, given that they will have much experience to share with the other candidates.

Reasons for reception

A person's desire to be received into the Church of England may stem from personal pragmatic reasons such as a change in the family's situation; it may come from a preference in style of worship or fellowship in the local church; it may come from a disagreement with the other church locally, nationally or internationally.

Where somebody simply wants to be included in the life of the local church but does not particularly want to move on from their previous denominational affiliation it may not be necessary for them to be formally received into full membership. The Church of England offers a welcome at Holy Communion to anybody who has been admitted to communion in another Christian church. Also, the Church of England Representation Rules make provision for baptized people in good standing with other churches to be included in the church's decision-making. They simply sign a declaration when applying for membership of the electoral roll:

> 'I am a member in good standing of a Church (not in communion with the Church of England) which subscribes to the doctrine of the Holy Trinity and also declare myself to be a member of the Church of England and have habitually attended public worship in the parish for at least the past six months.'
>
> [Church Representation Rules 1(2) (Appendix 1)]

Baptized and confirmed members of other churches in the Anglican Communion do not need to be received into membership of the Church of England. Baptized members of churches that have subscribed to the Porvoo Declaration are also regarded as members of the Church of England.

The Porvoo Churches have agreed to a common statement. The name comes from Porvoo Cathedral in Finland where the Eucharist was celebrated during the conversations that led to the statement. The Porvoo Churches are currently:

The Estonian Evangelical-Lutheran Church
The Church of Sweden
The Church of Norway
The Scottish Episcopal Church
The Church of Ireland
The Church of England
The Evangelical-Lutheran Church of Lithuania
The Church in Wales
The Evangelical-Lutheran Church of Iceland
The Evangelical-Lutheran Church of Finland
The Lusitanian Catholic Apostolic Evangelical Church of Portugal
The Spanish Episcopal Reformed Church

In the heady days of rapidly growing ecumenical relations around 1990s Liverpool the bishops preferred reception from other denominations to take place in a low key way during the regular Sunday worship of parish churches. Whilst *Common Worship* allows for reception as part of the confirmation service, this is not necessary. Where reception *is* part of a high-profile episcopally led service it is especially important that there is no sense of celebration at the expense of another church. This runs the risk of running down a candidate's past as well as being inappropriate to the Christian Church.

If the person being received is a priest from a non-Anglican church, the reception must be performed by the diocesan bishop or the bishop's representative.
(See Canon B 28.3)

'The candidates for confirmation who have previously been baptized (together with those affirming their baptismal faith or seeking reception) may come forward to the font and sign themselves with water, or the bishop may sprinkle them.'

Rubric from the Confirmation service, *CWCI*, p. 117

Differentiation

It is normally desirable for as little differentiation as possible to be made between different candidates in a single service of reception, as this provokes questions about why one person was treated differently from another.

The liturgy of initiation includes a number of elements. Candidates for reception should be encouraged to see the majority of this as appropriate to them and not simply their own declarations and reception. It is important for them, as for all candidates, that they be reminded of their own baptism and confirmation where these have taken place at another time in their lives.

Fonts

This chapter is about practicalities. It also presents suggestions for making full use of the dramatic possibilties the font provides as the focal centre of the Baptism service, the point towards which people turn or to which a procession moves, symbolizing the movement from darkness to light.

Using the position of the font

The Introduction to *CW Christian Initiation* makes suggestions for how this movement could be emphasized using lighting: 'Movement from darkness to light may be implied in the texts but can be realized in changing the lighting patterns in the building.' This will not be possible in every building, especially when strong daylight is coming into the building. However, this principle of marking a movement, and of seeing the font as an important symbolic place in its own right, can be applied in other ways. For example, when a worship space is being designed or reordered, floor texture or colour around the font can be given a different look or texture. If there is a choice in the matter, careful consideration can be given to the size and positioning of the font within the building. ➤

Canon F 1.2 states: 'The font shall stand as near to the principal entrance as conveniently may be … and shall be set in as spacious and well-ordered surroundings as possible.'

In this position, the font symbolizes entry into the faith, and is a reminder to every Christian entering the building of that time when they moved from darkness to light.

However, there is another matter to be taken into consideration on the position of the font in Canon B 21: 'It is desirable that every minister having a cure of souls shall normally administer the sacrament of Holy Baptism on Sundays at public worship when the most number of people come together, that the congregation there present may witness the receiving of them that be newly baptized into Christ's Church, and be put in remembrance of their own profession made to God in their Baptism.'

This might mean a fairly large congregation at the main service of the day, possibly too many to move to a position standing round a font in the doorway, especially if that is in one corner of the building. This is why some people consider using a small portable glass or stainless steel font, which can be moved to the front (or some other accessible and visible place) when required.

'[W]herever possible all candidates should make the profession of baptismal faith (even when there are no candidates for baptism) at the place of baptism, the font.'

Note 1, *CWCI*, page 128

➤**D7**

Some canticles and two litanies are provided in CW Christian Initiation (page 169ff.) for use in a procession to the font, but in many churches the use of hymns or worship songs will be more appropriate. [D8] The key is that music accompanying action can greatly heighten the sense of something significant happening, and prepare the congregation for a high point in the service.

Small bowl or pool?

This gives rise to a further pressing issue: the amount of water to be used. If we picture the three-fold symbolism of the water in baptism, pointing to birth and life, to death and drowning, and to washing and bathing, then each of these involves more than the few drops of water available from a sugar-bowl font. So Note 12 to the Baptism Service (page 100) says 'The use of a substantial amount of water is desirable; water must at least flow on the skin of the candidate.' So some mission-minded churches take the whole congregation to the sea, to the local swimming pool, or to another church for baptisms. This can be a powerful picture, a strong evocation of their own baptism and an opportunity to re-affirm it. Others have wanted to celebrate baptisms by immersion or submersion in the church itself, where other baptisms are celebrated. A large paddling pool can be used – preferably without dolphin and mermaid pictures on it! Another possibility is a birthing pool, as used for water births – very appropriate! If the imported pool is placed near to the church's font (or water is actually poured from the font into the pool) then a powerful link is made.

Guidance from the House of Bishops

A House of Bishops paper helpfully addresses these issues. *Response by the House of Bishops to Some Questions Raised By Diocesan Chancellors* (1992) has not had the publicity it deserves, although every diocese should have a copy. The chancellors are clearly told not to allow more than one font per church, even on a temporary basis, because of the potential for pastoral confusion about the unity of baptism, in appearing to give consumer choice and possibly in driving a wedge between 'christening infants' and 'baptizing adults'.

The paper suggests, at least for new churches, designing a font

> 'in which people can be baptized easily either by affusion (pouring of water over the head), immersion (pouring of water over the whole body, only parts of which are submerged) or, with careful management, submersion (placing as much as possible of the body under the water). This sort of design owes a good deal to models of the patristic and early medieval eras and is making something of a comeback today ... It safeguards the "one font" principle ... Where such a font is not practicable or

acceptable, an alternative might be a dignified font, large enough for affusion, standing over a pool large enough for immersion or submersion with steps leading in and out. The pool would need to be kept covered when not in use for reasons of safety, cleanliness and aesthetics. Such an alternative approximates to the one font rule.'

A third option, where one already exists, is to give:

'an historic font ... a spacious setting with an appropriate surrounding floor pattern to enhance its significance in the church and to enable more substantial quantities of water to be poured over a candidate before draining away through the redesigned floor.'

In some new buildings, such as the Roman Catholic cathedral in Bristol or the church of St Luke in Buckfastleigh, where the entrance is towards the front of the church, a stream flows from there to the font, which is situated where the congregation can easily see what is happening. This solution could be combined with one of the options described above.

Experiments have been made with different options for the shape of a sunken font. One, in the shape of a coffin, is symbolic both of Christ's death (into which we are baptized) and of our own. Others echo fourth-century examples, where an octagonal shape pointed to the 'eighth day', the day of resurrection and new creation, and a hexagonal shape to the sixth day, the day of crucifixion.

There is no ancient symbolic reason for the very common round shape, which probably comes from fonts originally being simply pools in the ground. But there is great variation in size. The first font at St John Lateran in Rome in the fourth century was 8.5 metres wide and a metre deep. The octagonal baptistery built to house it in the next century, the first and for some decades the only one in Rome, a prototype for other baptisteries, was big enough to accommodate the large numbers of adults being prepared for baptism by immersion.

Times have changed, and though no one builds baptisteries nowadays, the visual importance they gave to baptism is still worth recapturing in the prominence given to the font in church. And the expectation that adults, in small or large numbers, might be prepared in groups for baptisms at particular seasons of the year, is built into the preparatory rites in *CW Christian Initiation*.

Initiation and schools

Although this chapter is about *Church* schools, some of what is described may apply in places where a good *informal* relationship has been built up between school and church.

What experiences of Christian initiation are possible in Church of England schools? The answer must vary with the school and with the willingness of the staff and the local church to be involved, but there is potential for reaching whole families through the offer of baptism and confirmation services. In Church schools whole-school acts of worship are likely still to be happening, and many will include at least a termly celebration of Holy Communion. Here there is an opportunity for encouraging children to consider their own response to Christ. Fewer parents are having their children baptized as infants, often so that 'they can make up their own mind when they are old enough'. Here is a point at which that can happen.

All Church of England schools have links with their local church; some have weekly visits from ministers to lead an assembly, others have chaplains (who may or may not be ordained) who play both a liturgical and a pastoral role; many hold services in the parish church, especially at festivals or for a regular termly visit. Some schools, especially secondary schools, have a Christian Union (or similar group) at which issues of faith can be explored by pupils among their peers. Any of these situations can lead to conversations about what Christians believe, questions which can be answered in a different way to that laid down in the teaching syllabus.

What about the parents?

Some primary schools encourage parents to attend school services; be open to the possibility that some of these parents might be moved to take new steps of faith! Could a local church run an enquirers group or Alpha course nearby, ending at a convenient time for collecting children from school?[E2]

It can be tempting to take any enquiry about baptism or confirmation and deal with it through the parish on an individual basis. However, this means that the experience of initiation is not witnessed by the young person's peers. Some people argue that the school at worship is a church, and that initiation is into that body. But it is not necessary to go as far as that to ensure that those baptized are encouraged to relate to each other as a group, to seek support and encouragement from their contemporaries, and to invite them and others from school to their baptism. How much more positive for the children at a Church primary school to see one of their contemporaries being baptized, than to have a baptism enactment using a doll or teddy bear!

There is often a tradition within Church schools of having children confirmed at a certain point in their school career. In primary schools this may happen with top juniors (year 6), and may involve most or all of the class. Preparation can happen in school time (or immediately after school) and if there are sufficient candidates it may be possible for the Confirmation service itself to happen in school, with a visit by the bishop. One of the obvious hazards here is that confirmation is seen as part of the 'passing-out parade' from primary school, and all habits of collective worship can be lost on transfer to the local state comprehensive.

Another traditional age for confirmation, this time in secondary schools, is about 13 years old. Parental expectation sometimes plays a part here, with memories of being 'done' at a similar age. At this age there is less likelihood of a quick falling away, as the habit of collective worship will continue as long as the child is at school, but peer pressure in the middle-school years (age 14-15) makes it hard to continue to express Christian faith openly.

Young people are perhaps most likely to stay with their faith if their journey begins as a sixth-form enquirer. They are approaching adulthood, and with the prospect of leaving home for work or for university are beginning to think through their beliefs and to formulate a 'rule of life' or code of conduct. They have the confidence to withstand pressure, whether from peers or parents, and the maturity to realize that they are making a decision that will last into adult life.

We might want to question, however, the practice of inviting children who are still at school to make realistic promises of the type that are asked at confirmation. In parishes in which admission to Holy Communion before confirmation is becoming the norm, Church primary schools may become one of the places where children can receive some preparation prior to admission. In these situations confirmation can more easily be delayed until the later teenage years – when it can better fulfil its role as opportunity to affirm an adult faith for the future.

There are more children in our schools on Mondays than worshippers in our churches on Sundays (Dearing Report on Church Schools, 2001). If the school is there to serve the area, rather than to serve the church, a proportion of the children will not come from Christian backgrounds. While it is not the goal of the school to convert, we trust that many will be attracted to the faith of the Christians they encounter.

Handling initiation services

Baptism

Many children, even those at Church schools, will never have attended a baptism service. So if one of their contemporaries wishes to be baptized there is a wonderful opportunity for teaching and showing baptism in a practical way. The whole school can be invited, or just the candidate's closer friends and family; the service can happen in church or in school – or even outside school, if the child expresses a wish to be baptized by submersion or immersion. It can be easier to create imaginative liturgy outside the constraints of what is 'usual' in church. For the font:

- a portable font could be brought from the church;
- a paddling pool could be used for immersion, or for the liberal pouring of quantities of water;
- the baptism could take place in the school swimming pool, or other local facility.

D3 ➡ Within the liturgy ➡ full use can be made of all the permissions to omit and to use alternative texts. In particular:

- the Introduction can use 'other words' appropriate to the occasion;
- the Collect may be taken from the additional set of collects in simpler language;
- the Bible reading and Gospel could be dramatized;
- the Presentation of the Candidate may include a few words of testimony from the child;
- it may be felt that 'strong pastoral reasons' dictate that the alternative forms of the Decision and the Profession of Faith are used;
- the words of the Commission can be adapted to suit the occasion.

Making use of this flexibility can of course be just as appropriate in church as well as school contexts.

Confirmation

D12 ➡ Unless the bishop is prepared to visit the school, the liturgy of a confirmation service is probably influenced by the number, ages, and worship traditions of the others who are to be confirmed. Nevertheless, the school should be consulted ➡ in the arrangements to ensure that at least some of the hymns and songs are known by the candidates and the friends who come to support them. Might it be possible for the candidates to do the readings, or to help lead the prayers?

In the event that a school confirmation service is possible, some of the suggestions for baptism (above) also apply.

If a child who has not been baptized wishes to be confirmed, should both rites happen in the same service? Although having two separate services close together means that the child makes promises twice in quick succession, if the candidate is involved in two different worshipping communities (church and school) there may be value in having one community witness the baptism, and the other the confirmation.

Afterwards

Christian initiation is the opportunity for a celebration and a party. The facilities of a school offer the potential to invite baptism or confirmation candidates back to school for a party, or to continue the proceedings on site if the service has been held at school. The first communion for those baptized and admitted to communion, or those who have been confirmed, can also be an occasion to be marked in some way.

Most importantly, there needs to be some follow-through if initiation is really to be a beginning. ➤   ➤**E1 - E3**

- Does the school have a discussion or support group for new Christians? Or can the children be invited to join in a midweek group at the parish church?
- How can parents be encouraged to support the decision their child has made, and help them to attend worship regularly?
- Is worship within school 'going to church', or do we expect children to attend services more often than adults, by coming on Sundays as well as at school?

And one final issue ...

In an era when alternative expressions of church are being encouraged, should we see the Christian community that worships on school premises, during or after school hours, enjoying the sacraments of baptism and Holy Communion, as a congregation in its own right, rather than an adjunct to the parish church? In a 'mission-shaped church' situation this raises questions both of ecclesiology and of the extent to which mission, which is after all one of the marks of the baptismal church, can be allowable within the school context.

Section

C

C1 PREPARATION
Preparing adults for baptism

If we see baptism as a public commitment to follow Jesus, then we understand preparation for baptism as having two main tasks:

- explaining who Jesus is and what he has done for us;
- teaching about the life of a Christian disciple.

Preparation of the candidates is likely to focus on the intellectual dimension, but it is important to remember also:

- the spiritual dimension: their relationship with God
- the social dimension: their relationship with the congregation.

And so we need to consider the preparation of the church, not just the candidates.

- Is the community ready to welcome new members – some of whom might be from other social groups, or who might commit some liturgical or cultural *faux pas*?
- How will they fit into the existing structures for midweek fellowship, and how will they share in the ministry and leadership of the church?
- Is the building itself big enough to include significant numbers of new members?
- And if a church engaged in mission is expecting to see adult baptisms on a regular basis, should it have a built-in font large enough for immersion or submersion? ◄

B10 ◄

Who's coming?

A mission-shaped church may cast its net widely, or seek to witness to a particular social group. Nevertheless, those whose hearts are touched by God's Spirit will not be clones of one another, but come with a variety of experiences, abilities, motives, personalities, and attitudes. The leaders of a preparation course will find it a different and exciting process every time, even if they are working from the same syllabus or material.

Let's look more closely:

- **Experiences:** How widely have they travelled? How many different kinds of work have they done? Are they from small families or large, happy or less so? What education have they received?
- **Abilities:** What natural gifts and skills do they have? Do they have difficulties with learning, with mobility, with hearing or seeing? You may need strategies to deal with some of these differences in ability.
- **Motives:** At a human level, are they coming because of curiosity, loneliness, fear, joy, or something else?
- **Personalities:** Are they quiet and retiring, or bold and outgoing? Are they swayed more by their hearts or by their heads? You will have your own favourite way of characterizing personalities!
- **Attitudes:** Do they have a bone to pick with authority, with God or the Church? Are they eager or reluctant, anxious or joyful?

On the Way

The Church of England report, *On the Way* (1995), tried to integrate a number of aspects of Christian initiation. In the past people may have been baptized as infants, come to faith, and received some nurture in confirmation classes. Confirmation was their route to adult faith. The present mission situation suggests that this will not be the case for as many in the future and other approaches will have to be tried. One weakness of the old model is that the nurturing of faith was pastorally separated from the life of the congregation. People were not always introduced as candidates to the congregation, or prayed for regularly in services. If the confirmation was elsewhere, it did not influence many, who may not even have been aware that it was going on.

Steve and Sheila got interested in church through the birth of their first child, Polly. They started coming to the all-age Eucharist and enquired about baptism for Polly. Steve had been baptized as a child, Sheila was not baptized. The vicar suggested they join a preparation group. Also they were befriended by Marge, who runs the church's mums and toddlers group. They soon realized that they need to take further steps themselves and enquired about confirmation (including baptism for Sheila).

On the Way talks of five elements of Christian initiation:

1 **Church** – Initiation calls the Church:
   - to see itself as a baptized people
   - to welcome and learn from the enquirer
   - to be active in mission and service
   - to expect the anointing of the Holy Spirit
   - to walk with those seeking faith
   - to stand with the despised and oppressed
   - to look for the unity of God's people

2 Welcome – Enquirers need a welcome:
- that is personal
- that is public
- that accepts their starting point
- that expects the presence of God in their lives
- that is willing to travel with them at their pace

3 Prayer – Initiation involves prayer:
- for enquirer and Church
- to discern the presence of God
- to open up to the grace of God
- to support the process of change
- to discover the moments of decision
- to receive and recognize the gifts of God

4 The Way – Discipleship means learning:
- to worship with the Church
- to grow in prayer
- to listen to the Scriptures
- to serve our neighbour

5 Goal – The goal of initiation is:
- relationship with God the Holy Trinity
- life and worship with the Church
- service and witness in the world

CWCI, page 316

[See *CWCI*, page 193]

The church recognized that the preparation group was preparing for initiation, and they were welcomed before the whole congregation. Steve and Sheila found the group very helpful, and enjoyed the hospitality of members of the church as the group ate together as well as spending time in discussion. They committed themselves to getting baptized and confirmed at Easter. This commitment was marked by a brief ceremony in church some weeks before the baptism and confirmation, in which they received the sign of the cross. They noticed that their names, along with the rest of the group, were included in the prayers in church each week. In the group they particularly looked at the Four Texts, which they learned by heart, mostly through repetition and by singing. The baptism was a joyful event in the cathedral. Sheila and Polly were baptized and Steve and Sheila were confirmed. When they returned to church next Sunday they were welcomed into the congregation. The group continued as one of the home groups in the church. At Pentecost the whole congregation reaffirmed their baptismal commitment in the Corporate Renewal of Baptismal Vows.

The Four Texts
The Summary of the Law
The Lord's Prayer
The Apostles' Creed
The Beatitudes

Rites on the Way

In earlier centuries there was a complex initiation process, often called the Catechumenate. Adults (and their children) who wanted to be baptized may have spent years under instruction before being allowed to go forward for baptism. They then underwent intensive instruction, linked to prayer and liturgical rites that prepared them for baptism. Church members who vouched for their lifestyle accompanied them. In this process we find the origins of Lent and of godparents.

The catechumenate was revived by the Roman Catholic Church at the Second Vatican Council in the *Rite of Christian Initiation of Adults*. Such rites need careful pastoral application in the present Church, but we could learn much by integrating teaching, praying for people both in public in the liturgy and in private, and welcoming people by walking with them.

In the group of services named Rites on the Way, the Church of England offers a set of flexible resources to do this. The rites listed below provide a set of stages from an adult enquirer joining a group in preparation for baptism, through to preparing for the service of Baptism itself. Then other resources provide for the parish to welcome a person who has been baptized outside the parish. These services are not mandatory but need to be adapted to the local mission situation. They integrate a person's journey with the life of the church. Each takes a further step towards baptism and Christian commitment in the life of the church.

This material is in *CW Christian Initiation* (pages 29–56). Like all the other *Common Worship* services, it is available on the Church of England web site and as part of the *Visual Liturgy* service-planning software.

1. **Welcome of Those Preparing for the Baptism of Children** This is a short rite to welcome families into the church community, and can include godparents and sponsors as well as parents.

[Page 31]

2. **Welcome of Disciples on the Way of Faith** This is for people who have moved from initial exploration of the faith and now wish to journey on in exploration. It is intended as a public act and brings mission into the life of the community.

[Page 33]

3. **Affirmation of the Christian Way** This provides some brief responses reminding us that Jesus is the Way. It could be used in a small group or in church, possibly as part of the Welcome or the Call.

[Page 36]

4. **Call and Celebration of the Decision to be Baptized or Confirmed, or to Affirm Baptismal Faith** This is the moment of decision where people express their desire to be baptized, confirmed or affirm their faith. This would be a public act.

[Page 37]

5. **The Presentation of the Four Texts** The Four Texts are basic texts that give shape to our Christian life. They could also be particular areas to study or of preaching.

[Page 40]

6. **Prayers in Preparation for Baptism** This brief rite includes suggestions for readings and prayers that can be included in baptismal preparation or used on the eve of the baptism, either at home or in church.

[Page 48]

   The Resources section (pages 51-6) has a variety of suitable prayers which could be included: some are shorter and traditional, and some are longer, in responsorial form.

If candidates are baptized or confirmed outside the parish, there is provision to integrate the newly initiated in the local congregation:

Celebration after an Initiation Service outside the Parish These are resources to be used at a regular service.

[*CWCI*, page 182]

[*CWCI*, page 184] **Thanksgiving for Holy Baptism** This is a resource for the whole congregation to reflect on their baptismal faith with those recently baptized and commit themselves to further growth.

Rites on the Way showed how the different stages could fit in with the various liturgical seasons to reinforce the baptismal message [*CWCI*, pages 330-3] and life of the local church. It gave three models:

- **Pattern 1** Initiation at Easter
- **Pattern 2** Initiation at Epiphany / Baptism of Christ
- **Pattern 3** Initiation at All Saints

The pattern suggested for initiation at Easter, for example, builds up as follows:

Rite	Day
Call	The First Sunday of Lent
Presentation of the Four Texts	The Second, Third, Fourth and Fifth Sundays of Lent
Baptism, Confirmation (if bishop presides), Affirmation, Reception	Easter Vigil or Easter Day
Thanksgiving and Sending Out	Pentecost

The timing of the Welcome of Disciples on the Way of Faith (which would precede the Call, perhaps by several months) will depend on the length of the preparation envisaged.

> My confirmation was important to me. I did classes with the vicar, which I greatly enjoyed. We then went off to a church quite a way away and had a service with lots of other churches. We did not receive communion until we went back to our own churches. Nothing much was made of the confirmation, no prayers in church or introduction to the congregation.

The involvement of all the congregation

The model of initiation proposed here allows for the inclusion of many in the process of initiation of adults. This can include:

- hosts who can provide a place to meet and some food;
- intercessors in the church who pray for the candidates;
- people who meet with the candidates to befriend them;
- the preaching team who might preach a sermon series about baptism;
- the whole congregation who welcome and affirm those seeking baptism or confirmation.

It will also include:

- the vicar who oversees all the process and takes a part in the teaching; and
- the bishop who at some point welcomes the candidate to the life of the wider church.

This process therefore involves considerably more people than the traditional pattern confirmation classes held in churches, and it needs thinking through by the whole PCC. The aim is to draw in the entire congregation as an expression of their call to mission through baptism.

Courses for adult baptism preparation

A number of courses are used today for the preparation of adults for baptism. Some might be seen as *enquirers'* courses – designed for people who know very little about the Christian faith, but want to find out what it is about. People will pick up a holiday brochure for Mongolia, for example, before they have decided whether they want to go there: they need the information to help them decide.

Other courses are for *discipleship* – these are like the guidebook about Mongolia that travellers read after buying a ticket, in order to get the most out of the trip.

There will of course be some overlap in material. Something of the Mongolian landscape will feature in both the brochure and the guidebook, and something about the cross and resurrection is bound to feature both in an enquirers' course and in a discipleship course.

Not all courses are designed with baptism in mind, and some look for conversion without discussing baptism. All will need some adaptation to the local context. This process should also include consideration of how the course might be connected to Rites on the Way.

Some of the ideas in Chapter C3 will also apply to adult courses.

When reviewing the courses available, or designing a course specifically for local use, the church leadership team may want to prepare a checklist of the key ideas a candidate needs to live and grow as a Christian.

If you need inspiration you may find it in some of these:

- the Creeds;
- the Catechism in the 1662 *Book of Common Prayer*, and/or the Revised Catechism of 1962;
- the liturgy used in your church week by week;
- the Four Texts;

Chapter C6 provides a suggested checklist for confirmation preparation

Five Marks of Mission:

- To proclaim the Good News of the Kingdom
- To teach, baptize and nurture new believers
- To respond to human need by loving service
- To seek to transform unjust structures of society
- To strive to safeguard the integrity of creation and sustain and renew the life of the earth

- the Five Marks of Mission, as adopted by the Anglican Communion and other churches to guide their mission strategies.

If your checklist gets longer than a dozen ideas, divide them into two groups: the *essential* and the *desirable*. When it is ready, some of these questions may be helpful:

- If you are looking at an off-the peg course does it cover all your key ideas? If not, can you devise some extra sessions to make up for the deficiency?
- If your candidates are going to be confirmed some weeks after their baptism, which key ideas would you want to teach in that gap?
- Which key ideas are most important to convey to younger candidates?
- How will you know that the key ideas have been *grasped by the candidates*, and not just *taught by the course leader*?
- How will you encourage them to apply what they are learning? We are looking for *lives to be transformed*, as people grow in knowledge, faith and trust.
- Remembering that we are saved by our faith, not by our knowledge, would an inability to grasp some of the key ideas be a barrier to baptism?

As you plan to present the course you may also wish to consider:

- Will there be a balance of different modes of learning - for example, lecture, discussion, study of a text, action?
- Will there be a handout each time? And will it be given out at the beginning, to facilitate the learning, or at the end to summarize it?
- Are there some key ideas that might be better conveyed by a guest speaker or a trip?
- Will it be appropriate to set reading or other tasks to be done between sessions?
- Will there be opportunities for discussion? If you discover a 'burning' issue of importance to the course members, is there enough slack in your timetable to allow at least half a session on it?

We cannot expect preparation courses to cover everything. Learning and growth should go on throughout a Christian's lifetime - and this last expectation should be clearly conveyed by the course!

Preparing a family for Christian baptism

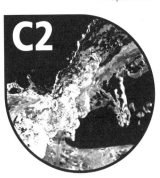

The Visit

It was early evening when I rang the door bell of number 17 and was greeted by a friendly smile: 'Come on in! The children are asleep.'

Melissa and Richard had been coming to church for about 18 months since the baptisms of Fiona (now aged five) and Peter (almost two); this was the first time I had visited them at home. We chatted over a glass of wine about life and work, Fiona's new school, and coping as parents of young children at church. Baptism preparation had made them think about what they believed and what they were doing.

There were three things they most remembered: first, the mum who came and talked about having her children baptized, about being baptized herself, and of the difference God made to her life; second, how important the promises were that they would be making; and third, that Christianity was not just a Sunday thing. Richard told me of his delight in praying with their children, how they didn't manage it every day but how they used the 'Thank you ... Sorry ... Please' pattern they had learnt in baptism preparation.

Family visits like this one are the exception rather than the norm. Most infant baptisms do not result in the family becoming regular worshippers – though some may attend for special occasions: Christmas, Mothering Sunday and Harvest. How do we respond to this?

►B2

One response is to limit baptism to those families who are already committed worshippers. A second is to create a series of hoops for people to jump through before they can have their children baptized. A third route is to see baptism preparation as a mission opportunity and to invest in it the time, money and spiritual capital of other mission initiatives and accept that this involves both risk and trust.

In preparing a family for a Christian baptism we need to engage with the parents on a number of different levels.

Engaging with the family

Emotional engagement

This can begin at a number of starting points. Parents begin to see that there are people who are genuinely interested in their child and who, like them, want the best for her. There may be the realization that those leading the group are Christian but 'normal' - perhaps in a similar stage of life to themselves, with children and similar experiences. Positive emotional engagement develops so that the parents do not just see the group as something they go to week by week, but as 'church'. As relationships develop and experiences are shared on the journey together, some will acknowledge that something is missing from their lives.

'What made you become a Christian?'
'I met Christians who had something I didn't have, that was good, and I wanted to share what they had.'

'But how are they to call on one in whom they have not believed? And how are they to believe in one of whom they have never heard? And how are they to hear without someone to proclaim him?'

Romans 10.14

Intellectual engagement

Most people do not know much about Christianity. One of the challenges that baptism preparation brings us face to face with is the need for a contemporary apologetic: an ability to communicate for today a knowledge and understanding of what Christianity is about. There will need to be some hard thinking about how best to use the time available and which topics are the key ones to look at.

Spiritual engagement

For many today, Church and organized religion may not be perceived as 'spiritual' at all. It is important that preparation includes time for reflection and prayer. The process is not about learning enough to understand what baptism is all about. It is about experiencing, possibly for the first time, the living God. It is about setting in place the foundations of an ongoing relationship that will grow through reading scripture, gathering for worship, receiving communion and living the Christian faith.

It's not about asking what the family will do for the church, but showing what God can do through the church for the family.

One danger in baptism preparation is that the focus is on what the Church expects and on the responsibilities of parents - and that God gets missed out.

Key issues and concerns

Issues we might be concerned about in preparing a family would include:

- establishing a relationship with the couple;
- demonstrating the Christian life and lifestyle;
- explaining the service and the promises involved;
- presenting the Christian gospel.

Issues they might be concerned about could include:

- Can I bring my baby or do I have to find a babysitter?
- What if the baby cries or needs a change?
- Do we both have to be there? Why?
- Will I have to talk, or meet people I don't know?

Before we can begin to address the issues that *we* are concerned with, it is vital to address the concerns and needs of those attending. Some can be addressed before people get to the group with helpful and friendly letters that answer the frequently-asked where, when, and how questions about what is going to happen.

Reasons people choose to have their children baptized

One church asks people about their reasons for having children baptized – it makes a good ice-breaker to start conversations. Some answers:

- 'I want him to learn what is right and wrong, and think that church will help.'
- 'I was baptized and I want the same for my child.'
- 'I want her to be able to be married in church.'
- 'It will enable us to celebrate her birth.'
- 'I hope she will go to Sunday school and learn about God.'
- 'It is important to belong to a religious faith.'
- 'The grandparents have been nagging us to have him done.'
- 'If he isn't baptized and anything happens I wouldn't forgive myself.'
- 'I want her to know the security of a personal relationship with God.'
- 'It might help him sleep better at night.'

Baptism preparation courses for families

As our nation moves from being a geographically-based society to a network-based society, there is increasingly less chance that those coming for baptism will see any points of connection between their network and church. With the shrinking of residual knowledge about the Christian faith, baptism preparation is often for parents who know very little about Christian faith. Yet still they come! The mission potential of such interest should be used and not wasted.

There are a number of important questions for a baptism preparation team to consider when planning a programme of preparation.

Where should the preparation be done, and for how many at a time?

At the parents' house

Advantages

- safe territory for the parents;
- parents don't have to organize babysitters or bring the child with them;
- gives the visitor an insight into the shape of family life;
- provides an opportunity to develop a relationship;
- means the preparation can be geared to the specific needs and issues of the particular parents;
- may make it easier to involve the godparents in the preparation.

Disadvantages

- limits contact to the one or two people making the visit;
- not always the best environment for discussion, as a baby or young children can be either a distraction or a good way for the parents to avoid key issues;
- can also present practical difficulties (I remember visiting a couple at home, with whom I had checked in advance that they had a video player; when it came to time to show the video, they explained that their video player was in the bedroom!);
- involves very little effort on behalf of those asking for baptism; they simply have to be at home, and some do not even turn off the television.

At the church hall/church

Advantages

- usually plenty of space so it is possible to have larger groups (which may be important if you have lots of enquiries and a small team to do the preparation);
- familiarizes those attending with the space and may help them feel more comfortable coming to Sunday school, crèche or toddler groups;
- gives parents the chance to meet others who are in a similar situation.

Disadvantages

- the space may not be very attractive, comfortable, or appropriate;
- parents have to organize childcare (or the church has to provide it);
- a bigger group may make it harder for nervous participants to contribute;
- can feel too much like an evening class – people may mistakenly assume an emphasis on needing to learn enough to qualify.

At a congregation member's or clergy home

Advantages
- a home is comfortable;
- refreshments are easy to organize – more natural to offer a glass of wine or fruit juice in the intimacy of home rather than in the formality of the church hall;
- if it is the home of parents of small children it will be child-friendly.

Disadvantages
- unless someone has a particularly large lounge it is difficult to gather more than a few couples;
- some participants may feel awkward about coming to the home of someone they don't know;
- affects the rest of the members of the household;
- involves time in getting the room ready and clearing away afterwards.

In terms of the numbers to involve, three or four couples with four congregation members can work well:

- one person hosts;
- one leads the session;
- one does the administration, meets and links with the families when they come to church; and
- the fourth is someone who has been through the course, and is now part of church.

Should the infant be in attendance?

For
There is a natural logic in parents bringing the children along, and children offer a natural way to start conversation. It is also important to send the right signals to parents that the church welcomes children.

Against
The children can become a distraction or a way of avoiding things. There may be practical hurdles such as baby-feeding and changing. Evening sessions can disrupt bedtime.

The most important conversations often take place after the formal session – if parents are worrying about getting the children home they are less likely to stay.

How often should we meet?

A single session has the advantage for those attending that they only have to arrange babysitters (or welcome baptism visitors) for the one occasion. It also means that the church can concentrate resources. Parents of small children are busy people and some will find it difficult to attend a number of meetings, or to get back from work in time.

The advantage of meeting over several sessions is that there is the opportunity for relationships to develop and deepen; the dynamic changes, and the quieter and shyer participants are more likely to share their views. It also makes activities between sessions possible, most notably to make use of the material in the Welcome of Those Preparing for the Baptism of Children. It may also give participants the opportunity to see a baptism service.

[Page 31]

Some patterns of preparation

Model A	Model B	Model C
Week 1 First Session	*Week 1* Sunday Church (Welcome of Those Preparing for the Baptism of Children)	*Week 1* Session 1 including (Welcome of Those Preparing for the Baptism of Children)
Week 2 Second session		
Week 3 Sunday Church: experience of a Baptism service	*Week 2* First Session	*Week 2* Session 2
	Week 3 Second session	*Week 3* Session 3
Week 4 Third session	*Week 4* Sunday Church experience of a Baptism service	*Week 4* Sunday Baptism
Week 5 Sunday Church (Welcome of Those Preparing for the Baptism of Children)		
	Week 5 Third session	
Week 8 Baptism	*Week 8* Baptism	

An important consideration is at what point in the process to use the Welcome of Those Preparing for the Baptism of Children. In Model A the rite comes at the end of the three preparation sessions and after seeing a Baptism service, when the parents know what they are preparing for. There has been the opportunity to explain ideas of journey and formation before the family is invited to participate in the rite. The focus is on their preparation - it sees Christian formation as a process and moves away from the idea of baptism preparation as a test that they need to pass before they are allowed to graduate and have the baptism itself.

Model B uses the rite as the initial activity of the course of preparation and this may act as a filter for parents not sure why they are coming to church or what they are coming for. The danger is that it may filter parents on grounds of character and determination rather than spiritual need.

Model C offers the rite in the context of the first preparation session. The disadvantage of this is that only a small sample of the wider congregation - the baptism preparation team - is present to welcome, support and pray for the families.

Sample course content

A carefully constructed preparation course requires a variety of presentation methods and types of input.

Ice-breakers

Opening activities give everyone the opportunity to talk and be listened to. In larger groups the opportunity to move around helps to build confidence and group relationships. See the sample ideas in the margin box.

Audio-visual material

There are some useful video resources available for baptism preparation. Take a look on the Internet or in your Christian bookshop. Some churches produce their own videos or DVDs of actual or re-staged baptisms – these can be used to look at the service in more detail and talk through the individual parts. A home-produced resource can also contain testimony, worship samples and information about groups and activities as well as teaching material about baptism. Home-produced DVDs and videos have the advantage that they can be cheaply reproduced and given to families to watch at home and keep.

PowerPoint® presentations (useful for looking at key themes, the outline of the service and the wording of the promises), television and film clips can reinforce some of the ideas and concepts.

An advantage of using DVDs and videos is that it enables group leaders to ask different sorts of questions and stand back from the issues raised. For example: 'The video talked about Jesus dying for our sins, what does that mean for us here today?' 'The video made it sound easy to bring your children to church; what is it like for you?'

Bible study

This gives opportunity for those in preparation to read at first hand the accounts of baptism in the New Testament. It is important for each person to have a copy of whatever passages are being used.

Discussion

Giving opportunity for parents to share with others in a similar situation builds up confidence and draws out ideas, questions and worries that may not otherwise be shared in the large group. Simple discussion cards which people pick up in turn can facilitate this.

Ice-breakers

Why have you chosen the names that you have for your child? This often leads into discussion of being part of a family, of personal history, and of individuals that have influenced us – all of which can be applied directly to the Christian faith and life.

Why do you want to have your child baptized? This could be done by giving out a sheet with possible reasons for seeking baptism for a child, and inviting them to choose their top two or three reasons for choosing baptism.

Signature Bingo Participants have a card each and talk to others, who sign their card if they match certain criteria (like being an only child, playing an instrument, etc.).

Some passages to study:

Acts 16.13-15
Acts 16.22-36
John 3.1-21
Romans 6.1-7

For more ideas, see *CW Christian Initiation*, page 323 and pages 150–65.[see also D4]

Some discussion questions

What do you like most about Jesus?

When do you find you pray with your child?

How will your child's baptism change your life?

Do you feel closer to God now than when you were 12?

What makes going to church difficult for you?

Questions

Create an atmosphere where *all* questions are welcome. Providing paper and pens for people to jot questions, thoughts, things to ask and things to do may help.

Testimony

Parents who have had their children baptized recently, come to a new stage in their faith and become integrated into the life of the church will have a powerful impact when given the opportunity to share their story. The personality and the gifts of the individual will determine whether a question and answer approach or just telling their story is best.

Activities at home

Preparation is not just about what happens in the group but also about applying and reflecting upon what happens at home. Exploring what it means to live as a Christian family is a good basis for activities outside the preparation sessions. This could include:

- Shaping the day: looking at bedtime prayers, Christian books and activities, mealtimes and grace, home rituals.
- Shaping the week: the importance of Sunday worship, taking time together as a family, welcoming guests.
- Shaping the year: making the most of festivals and seasons to re-tell our Christian story. What do we do that makes Christmas or Epiphany, Lent or Easter or Advent special? How do we mark birthdays, baptism anniversary, starting school?

Prayer

Prayer is far more than the start and finish of each meeting for preparation. Prayer is inviting God into the process before the first meeting. Prayer is a way of inviting the congregation into the **C6➤** preparation process. ➤ As they pray for those who are going to begin preparation it is their own hearts as well as those they are praying for that are changed.

Prayer times in the preparation sessions need to be real and vital, and could include times of open prayer, asking people to share prayer needs, praying for the children to be baptized, leaving space and quiet for God to speak. Prayer in the meeting can include using [*CWCI*, page 48] a simple liturgy such as Prayers in Preparation for Baptism or using a mixture of stillness, open prayer, quiet music or song, lighting candles, short reading from Scripture.

Preparing godparents and sponsors

C3

The distinction between godparents and sponsors was made in Chapter B7. ➛ Most of what follows applies to sponsors as well as to godparents.

➛B7

What does being a godparent involve?

In the questions to parents in the Baptism service, there is a clear expectation that that they intend to bring their child up to be a Christian and an active member of the local church. The church congregation has a role to play in this, but the greater responsibility for making sure that the child learns about the Christian faith and takes the appropriate place in the church community lies with the godparents.

The service does not demand (or expect) that the godparents will have the answer to every question, or every issue. It sees baptism as the start of a lifelong journey - godparents and sponsors are there to encourage and support the candidate on that journey. What is needed is a basic belief, and a willingness to journey and learn together. This journeying can develop into a most fruitful spiritual relationship for all those involved.

Preparing for the Baptism service

At several points in the service the godparents take a spoken or active part. To see how this fits in they will need some overall understanding of what the service is about and how the structure works. ➛ What the godparents do and say can be used as part of the preparation for the service, to ensure that they understand the role that they have agreed to undertake.

➛D3

In the course of the service godparents make promises for themselves or on behalf of the child.

They respond to the love of God:

- they promise to take a special interest in their godchild, and in his or her Christian development;
- they undertake to pray regularly for the child and the family;

N and N, you have been asked to nurture *these children* as they grow in faith.

May God bring you joy as you hold *them* in his love,
and walk with *them* on the Way of Christ.
May you be a blessing to one another,
and may the blessing of God almighty,
the Father, the Son and the Holy Spirit,
be among you and remain with you always. Amen.

CWCI, page 32

C2

Becoming a Godparent (Church House Publishing, 2003) outlines the short- and longer-term role and responsibilities of godparents; describes what happens in a Baptism service, and suggests suitable baptism gifts. *Your Child's Baptism* (Church House Publishing, 2003) provides guidance to parents on what happens at a baptism, what decisions they will be asked to make, what role the godparents play and what will happen during the service.

- they promise, by their example, to encourage the child to go to church, to learn about Christ, and ultimately come to confirmation; and
- in anticipation of all this the whole congregation prays for them at the Commission.

They may also take a more active part in the service:

- they may be invited to present the child to be baptized;
- they may mark the child with the sign of the cross after the Decision;
- they may dress the child in white after the baptism;
- they may receive the lighted candle on the child's behalf towards the end of the service.

It is best if godparents can be part of any preparation with the parents. This may not be possible if they live some distance away. However, if the preparation can include a run-through of the service or a rehearsal in church (which could be held the day before the baptism), then some may be able to be present and involved in at least part of the process.

Preparation for far-flung godparents

Godparents who are not able to attend the preparation could be sent some of the material that is used, or maybe a video, along with a copy of any parish leaflet about baptism, and a copy of the service itself, with their part clearly marked.

A booklet or leaflet for godparents

This might cover the following topics:

What is being a godparent about?

This could address issues such as:

- the privilege of being a godparent;
- what the requirements are for a godparent.

What are you promising to do?

This could include preparation material based on the service itself, for example:

- the practical consequences of the commitments made at the Presentation;
- the meaning of the promises made at the Decision;

- the significance of any symbolism to be used in the service (water, the sign of the cross, the light of a candle, anointing with oil, clothing in white and so on)➤

➤D7

Where do I go from here?

This could give new godparents ideas about developing a relationship with the child, such as:

- giving books of prayers or a Bible suitable for the age, at various points in their godchild's life;
- marking the anniversary of baptism instead of (or as well as) the birthday;
- writing letters;
- praying, maybe using any prayer card given at the Baptism service.➤

➤E1 – E3

When does my responsibility come to an end?

Ideally, godparents should be encouraged to develop a lifelong relationship with their godchild, even if the promises seem to be fulfilled when a child is confirmed.

Many children develop a special relationship with their godparents, that lasts long into adulthood. 'My spinster godmother got married when I was about 30. I was really excited, which surprised us both, and showed me that our relationship was closer than I had thought.'

Relationship with the parents

The role covers supporting the parents as well as the child, so that the whole family grows in a relationship with God.

Prayer

It is good to include in the booklet a suggested prayer for regular use.

Questions for discussion

1. What is your current pattern of preparation for the parents of those to be baptized? Is there any way that you could change it to make it easier to involve godparents or sponsors?

2. Is there any way that you could offer ongoing support to godparents? Ideas could include sending them material at the anniversary of their godchild's baptism, or inviting them to an annual service specially for godparents.

C4 Preparing children for admission to Holy Communion

The focus for preparation for admission to Holy Communion should be primarily on growing in understanding of the Eucharist (at a level which is appropriate to the child's age) and being able to participate more fully in it. The temptation to present a mini-confirmation course, covering a full curriculum of Bible, prayer, ethics, stewardship etc. should be resisted. These things are important – by all means let them be covered in the normal children's ministry within the church – but let the preparation for communion focus on communion itself. In particular, it is vital to remember that children are admitted to communion on the basis of their baptism and their participation in the life of the church – *not* on the basis of reaching some specific level of knowledge or understanding about the Eucharist. When the decisions about whether a child is ready to be admitted come to be taken, it is vital to make sure it doesn't feel like some sort of exam which the child has to pass in order to be able to receive communion.

Practical factors to consider

B8➤ The Admission to Holy Communion Regulations (2006) ➤ make it clear that before a bishop gives permission for children to be admitted in a particular parish, there will need to be consideration of how the children will be prepared. The practicalities will vary according to local factors:

- How many children are being admitted?
- What age are the children?
- How will the parents be involved?

How many children?

In the first year of the new policy, a church is likely to have a bigger group of children, and of more widely varying ages, than in succeeding years. Preparation for a dozen children is obviously going to be different to preparing one or two children. In the former case, a series of special classes or groups will be an obvious model that may work, with two, three or more adult leaders.

Much published material assumes this sort of model, but it may need adjusting if numbers are smaller. With just one or two children, it may be more appropriate to give the children some activities to

As with all preparation or group work involving children, don't forget to make sure the church's Child Protection policy is adhered to. Though preparation groups will be temporary (compared to ongoing children's work), Child Protection should be applied in exactly the same way.

work on at home with their parents and at church, and then to arrange to visit the child (and parents) in his or her own home to talk through what has been discovered.

What ages are the children?

A group of 5- or 6-year-olds will clearly need a different approach to a group of 9- or 10-year-olds. The bishops' regulations do not specify a minimum age for admission to communion, though the bishop may establish such boundaries within a particular diocese. In practice it often pays to be flexible, determining each child's readiness (or not) in discussion with the child and his or her parents. The minimum age set by a bishop might be, say, 5 years old, but a particular child might benefit from waiting a little longer before starting preparation.

If the spread of ages in the group is too great, then it may be wise to find some way of splitting the group and keeping children of similar ages together.

Whatever the age and number of the children it will be important to make sure that preparation includes the opportunity for children to reflect on their own experience of church and communion, as well as being 'taught' any particular understanding of what it means. Preparation for admission to communion is a great opportunity for adults to learn from children as well as vice versa.

[Younger children may benefit from talking through resources such as the *Holy Communion cube* (Church House Publishing, 2006).]

Leader: 'I wonder what it means in the service when the priest says, "Lift up your hearts"?' Seven-year-old: 'I think it means that we send our love to God.'

How will the parents be involved?

There will be three key stages at which parents can and should be involved:

Before preparation

Parents will need to be consulted and informed about the practice of the church and then enabled to see how they can help their children as they go through the preparation process. The process itself will need to be carefully explained, especially if parents are not familiar with admission to Holy Communion before confirmation. It needs to be clear that taking part in preparation does not mean a child *has* to be admitted, if child, parent or incumbent don't feel the child is ready.

During preparation

In some churches parents may be included in the preparation groups, working alongside their children. In other situations, where the children will be meeting without parents, parents can be involved by helping children with activities between meetings. It will be important to make this as little like school homework as possible, and to emphasize the sense of children and parents discovering together, rather than parents giving children 'the answers'.

After preparation

Parents will need to be involved in the decision about whether their child is ready for admission to communion, and helped to see how they can continue to support their child in being a communicant member of the church. It will also help if parents are invited to the preparation session at which practical aspects of receiving communion are discussed, so that they know what instructions have been given to their children, and can remind them (and perhaps practise) at home.

Key things to cover in preparation

There are several published courses to help with preparation, but they need to be adapted to the particular needs of the parish. Some parishes will be working from their own material. Whichever pattern is followed, these are some of the key issues to cover (not necessarily in this order):

- Communities in which we belong (family, church, school, clubs etc.) as places where we can receive God's love and share it with others.
- Eating and drinking together as ways of knowing and showing that we belong.
- Special food in our lives - birthday and wedding cakes, Christmas dinner, inviting people to eat with us, going out for a meal, and so on.
- Special meals in the life of Jesus - feeding miracles, eating with sinners, eternal life as heavenly banquet, the last supper, resurrection meals with the disciples.
- Baptism as the way we join the church and Holy Communion as a meal that shows we belong to Jesus and the Church.
- Different names for the service (Eucharist, Holy Communion, Mass, Lord's Supper) and the different emphases they bring.
- What happens in a Eucharist in our church - including talking about the different parts of the service and the words that are used.
- Showing the children the objects used in communion (bread, wine, chalices, plates, candles, and so on).
- Practical advice: how to hold your hands to receive the bread, how to hold the cup, saying 'Amen', what to do if you have a cold, how long to stay at the rail, and so on.
- A chance to taste the bread and wine as used in your church, ahead of the first time the child receives communion.

Questions for discussion

1. What are your memories of the first time you received communion?

2. How has your understanding of Holy Communion changed since then?

3. Does it matter to you that other people might understand Holy Communion in a different way?

4. Are there members of your church who could help with this preparation - perhaps regular communicants who don't have any other responsibilities with children or young people?

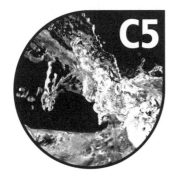

C5

Preparing for confirmation

Ryan and **Kate** had been coming to church regularly with their parents since they were children. When they were aged 17 and 15 they decided that they wanted to be confirmed. Their vicar arranged a series of weekly meetings with them and another couple of teenagers from their group of parishes. The sessions were based on an off-the-shelf preparation course, but were tailored to fit their particular needs. None of the teenagers had much Bible background, nor had they had the chance to discuss their faith in a group before, so they found the experience a bit scary at first. However, by the end of the course they were willing to open up more about their own ideas.

Claire and **Eleanor** were young mums who had become more involved with the church through their children's baptisms. They now wanted to know more about Christianity, and to belong to the church in a more formal way. They spent a few weeks meeting with some members of the youth group who wanted to be confirmed, in the vicar's home, and enjoyed watching a video to spark off discussion about how their faith had an effect on their daily lives. A dad who had been confirmed the previous year helped with the leadership of the sessions. The mix of teenagers and adults was a surprisingly fruitful one, and they all learnt from one another.

These examples show the benefits of being flexible over confirmation preparation. Different places, times, age groups, formats and resources will work in some contexts and not others, and anyone leading a group will need to know the members as well as the material which is going to be used. If your church has been preparing children for communion before confirmation, the areas covered in that preparation will also need to be borne in mind so that they can be built upon as necessary.

Resources available

C1, C3 ➜ These will obviously vary, but they all have different strengths and weaknesses, ➜ and you will probably find one course more useful for your particular group than another. Often you can mix and match ideas from different courses, and add in your own modifications too.

New material and courses are coming out all the time, so the best thing to do is to take a look in your local Christian bookshop, or search on the Internet, to see the full range that is available.

Don't forget that some of the most popular courses on the basics of Christianity are not written with confirmation specifically in mind, so you will need to supplement specific material if you wish to use them as a confirmation course.

What to include

What subjects need to be included in a confirmation course? Your ideas on this will be influenced by the particular focus put on confirmation in your church. If the emphasis is on adult commitment and service of Christ, you may want to include something on mission, serving Christ in practical ways in the world, and sharing your faith. If your candidates have a background in another denomination, you might want to include a bit more about Anglican doctrine and practice. If children are admitted to communion before confirmation in your church, then teaching about Holy Communion in the confirmation course will not be so central, and certainly will be handled differently compared with a church in which confirmation is still the gateway to Holy Communion. You will know your candidates and what they already know, but here is a checklist of the Christian basics and other things they will need to think about in order to grow as Christians:

- God – including God's role as creator;
- Jesus – incarnation, life, teaching, death and resurrection;
- Holy Spirit – giving courage, guidance, fruit and gifts;
- prayer – different patterns and kinds of prayer;
- the Bible – personal patterns for reading it; the varied kinds of writing, and different ways to interpret what we read;
- the church – unity and diversity, and the call for each us to use our gifts with others;
- Baptism and confirmation – their role in the life of the church;
- Holy Communion – practicalities; and different understandings of what is going on;
- sharing the faith in word and action;
- being a Christian at home, school and work.

Christian faith is of course a life to be lived, not an exam to be passed, and however a course is taught and shared, it is important to take on board the various experiences people bring with them. A course should equip those who take it to go on learning, both by themselves and with others, and to go on discovering other things along their journey. The style of teaching should therefore encourage individuals to discuss and investigate. You may find some of the courses available may not take account of the different ways people come to faith, and careful use of them is essential if people at different stages of the journey are to feel comfortable sharing their spiritual life with others.

Using the Confirmation service as a starting point – some ideas

- What does it mean to believe that 'God has called you by name and made you his own'?
- How can I expect to see the results in me of the Holy Spirit – the Spirit of 'wisdom and understanding'; 'counsel and inward strength'; 'knowledge and true godliness'?
- What does it mean to be 'faithful to our baptism' and 'ready for that day when the whole creation shall be made perfect in your Son'?
- Look at each section of the Commission (*CW Christian Initiation*, page 119). What are the implications for daily life in committing yourself to this?

C6⬩
C3⬩

[*CWCI*, pages 29-56]

Preparation for a life of discipleship will mean action as well as learning. Are there ways in which the confirmation preparation group can get involved in some Christian service together, either within the church or in the wider community?

It will also be useful to use the text of the Confirmation service itself as a source of study and reflection, and to help candidates to reflect on their experience of worship more generally.

In this way, they can begin to see worship as something that not only reflects and expresses their belief about God and relationship with God, but also *shapes* those beliefs and *deepens* that relationship. In many ways, confirmation preparation is therefore not so much about learning particular elements of the Christian faith, but establishing a pattern of Christian living in which learning, questioning, sharing, and reflecting are seen as central and lifelong.

Involving the church

The decision to be confirmed, though it may seem an individual one, is made within the context of the whole baptized people of God. Other members of the Body of Christ should therefore be involved. ⬩ On an individual level, they may be involved as supporters or sponsors ⬩ of those being confirmed, or they may help with the confirmation preparation. On a wider level, the provision of material in *CW Christian Initiation* of Rites Supporting Disciples on the Way of Christ means that some more public acknowledgement of the candidates' journey of faith can be made, and through this the congregation can be both encouraged and involved in supporting and praying for them. In addition, the Presentation of the Four Texts might be used as a link between subjects discussed in confirmation groups and Sunday worship.

Preparing for the Confirmation service
The practicalities

Much will depend on whether the service is being held in your own parish or at the cathedral or in another church in the benefice or
B3⬩ deanery. ⬩

If possible, it is good if the candidates can have some input into the service, whether that be in planning or taking part in the readings, prayers, testimony, or music. This obviously requires a lot of communication and planning well in advance between those responsible for organizing the service, so don't leave things until the last minute!

The spiritual part

Candidates and their clergy and families can get so immersed in the practical details of the service that any spiritual preparation can get overlooked. Perhaps, as well as the confirmation rehearsal, where there will be a chance to 'walk through' the service, there can be some time where the candidates can have some space for prayer and reflection.

Some suggestions:

- pizza and a chill-out zone before or after the rehearsal, with some ideas for prayer and a few worship songs;
- a meal and a chance to talk about spiritual issues, finishing with time for prayer and silence;
- in a larger context with more resources, perhaps the confirmation group could spend a day or a half-day away together on a mini-retreat – could the bishop be invited to come?

Something to remember

As the introduction to *CW Christian Initiation* stresses, confirmation is a part of the journey of faith in Christ, and does not stand alone. It would help good practice if all those involved in planning confirmation services and confirmation preparation kept in mind that confirmation can be part of the journey into the growth of new Christians, part of the nurture of disciples, part of the bigger story, both for each individual and for the church. As the quotation on page 9 of the Introduction says:

> 'The journey into faith involves a process that includes awareness of God, recognition of God's work in Christ, entering into the Christian story through the scriptures, turning to Christ as Lord, incorporation into the body of Christ, nurture within the worshipping community, and being equipped and commissioned for ministry and mission within God's world.'
>
> International Anglican Liturgical Consultation, Toronto, 1991

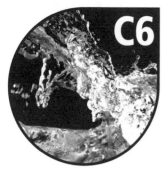

C6

A1, A4

The role of the wider congregation

Baptism is a corporate event, as well as an individual one. 'For we were all baptized by one Spirit into one body' (1 Corinthians 12.13 NIV) and 'each member belongs to all the others' (Romans 12.5 NIV), in a church with 'one Lord, one faith, one baptism' (Ephesians 4.5). Baptism is not just about individual vocation: it is part of our very identity as Christians that we are, together, in Christ. Therefore, in the underlying theology, words and actions in the Baptism service, and in the pre- and post-baptismal care of the candidate, the whole congregation should be an integral part of the individual's journey of faith. This congregational role was emphasized in the report *On The Way*, which encouraged lay involvement in the process from initial enquiry to faith formation and nurture, as well as in the Baptism service itself. None of the five elements of Christian initiation it identifies can be achieved without the wider Church:

- the church learns from the enquirer as it unfolds what it means to be the community of the baptized;
- the welcome given to enquirers depends on the church playing its part and being open to change;
- the enquirer's journey must be surrounded and undergirded by the church's prayers;
- the church must help the new member to learn to be a disciple through worship, prayer, engagement with Scripture and service;
- the goal is not only relationship with God and service to the world, but life and worship with the rest of the Church.

See Section C1, pages 91f. above. See also Gilly Myers, *Using Common Worship: Initiation* (Church House Publishing, 2000), pages 21-38.

Preparation for initiation

'Care and time needs to be taken to help a church understand that the welcome and nurture of new Christians is the responsibility of the whole people of God.'

On the Way, Chapter 11: Pastoral Implications, p. 112

B2

From enquiry to continuing life in the Church

Being a missionary church, with an expectation of new life and faith, will mean involving the whole Church leadership, lay and ordained, in the welcome and nurture of new Christians. The church council's role in establishing a baptism policy for the church lays the foundation, and teaching and visible participation of lay members of the congregation throughout the baptism process will support it.

Adult candidates

In the preparation of adults for baptism and confirmation, the sense of being fellow travellers on a journey is encouraged by group preparation and by the appointment of a designated member of the congregation to accompany the candidate through the process. That person could then act as the candidate's sponsor at the initiation service (if they have no-one else that they wish to ask) or could simply provide additional caring support throughout the process. ➤

➤**C3**

Support is also given by the public recognition of the candidates' journey in the main act of worship and in such rites as the Welcome of Disciples on the Way of Faith, Affirmation of the Christian Way, and Call and Celebration of the Decision to be Baptized or Confirmed, or to Affirm Baptismal Faith. ➤

➤**C1**

Infant candidates

In infant baptism the congregation has a role in welcome and encouragement of the whole family. This can include lay participation in baptism preparation sessions, in building relationships with the baptism family, and through any existing age-related groups for all the family members. Having a dedicated link person to each family preparing for a baptism is helpful, especially if this is continued throughout the process and into the years beyond. For example, baptism visitors (sometimes called 'baptism Aunts' or 'Uncles'), can visit in the early stages of contact, be present during baptism preparation sessions, have a role during the service itself, and be responsible for annual anniversary and birthday cards afterwards.

Support and training

The choice and preparation of those accompanying baptism candidates needs careful consideration. The gifting of individuals needs supporting by training and long-term supervision. Any role that may involve contact with children will also be subject to the usual safeguards of the church's Child Protection measures. A regular group-meeting for baptism visitors will give them the support they will need, and be an opportunity for assessing training and development needs and pastoral concerns.

Congregational role in the Baptism service

The timing of the service – some options

The preference for baptism to take place at the main service on a Sunday underlines the importance of the corporate aspect of the rite, and makes the sense of joining the church family stronger. ➤
However, where this is not possible and baptisms have to take place

Canon B 21 Of Holy Baptism
It is desirable that every minister having a cure of souls shall normally administer the sacrament of Holy Baptism on Sundays at public worship when the most number of people come together, that the congregation there present may witness the receiving of them that be newly baptized into Christ's Church, and be put in remembrance of their own profession made to God in their baptism.

➤**B5**

as separate services, the greater use of the service of Thanksgiving for the Gift of a Child, and of the Welcome from the Baptism service, can be helpful.

Thanksgiving for the Gift of a Child can take place in any service and does not need to dominate the whole service in the way that baptism does. It can be an informal and welcoming act for the parents and immediate family on a Sunday prior to the baptism. The Welcome from the Baptism service can then be deferred until a Sunday following baptism, giving an opportunity for the public recognition that the candidate has joined the regular worshipping community. ➔

B5 ➔

Congregational responses

Throughout the Baptism service the congregational participation and the underlying theology of the service expresses the importance of seeing baptism as being related to the whole body of Christ, not just the individual. There is more specific reference in:

May God, who has received you by baptism into his Church,
pour upon you the riches of his grace,
that within the company of Christ's pilgrim people
you may daily be renewed by his anointing Spirit,
and come to the inheritance of the saints in glory.
Amen.

CWCI, page 71

- the *Presentation of the Candidates*, where the congregation is asked if they welcome and will support the candidates;
- the *Profession of Faith*, which is introduced by asking the congregation to profess the faith of the Church together with the candidates;
- the *prayer* for the Spirit, that immediately follows the baptism, which acknowledges that the candidate has been received into the Church, and locates the new believer 'within the company of Christ's pilgrim people';
- the words of the *Commission*: 'they will need the help and encouragement of the Christian community ...';
- the *post-baptism prayers*, which include reference to the life-long journey that is made together with all God's people;
- the *Act of Commitment* for those old enough to answer for themselves, in which the first question underlines the importance of fellowship;
- The *Welcome and Peace*, which stress the corporate nature of the church and that the candidate has been baptized into one body, and is welcomed into the fellowship of faith.

In the actions there is also scope for emphasizing the role of the wider congregation. The specially designated support of sponsors and baptism visitors can be stressed if they stand beside the candidate(s) during the decision and baptism. The service rubrics say that the president may invite parents, godparents and sponsors to sign the candidates with the cross and that the president or another person may give each of the newly baptized a lighted candle. Using members of the congregation, church wardens or baptism visitors at any of these points can call attention to the oneness in Christ expressed in baptism.

Post-baptismal role

The continuing life of the baptized person as part of the Body of Christ - as a person sharing the journey with others as a fellow pilgrim - can be supported by post-baptismal rites such as Celebration after an Initiation Service outside the Parish, Thanksgiving for Holy Baptism or Admission of the Baptized to Communion. ☛ However the main incorporation is in the regular life ☛**B5, D9** of the church as part of the worshipping community and in the long-term nurture of faith. ☛ Through this the newly baptized person, ☛**E1** young or older, is equipped and encouraged for their life of discipleship and witness. They experience the love and care of a Christian community and learn to give of themselves to others within the Body of Christ and in the world.☛ ☛**E2 - E4**

Questions for discussion

1. Looking back to your own early years in the family of the Church, which people and what events made you feel part of the community?

2. And what helped you to grow in the faith?

3. What kind of people would make good baptism visitors or sponsors?

Section

D

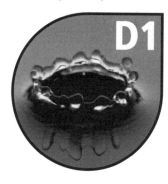

D1 SERVICES
Liturgy surrounding childbirth

Conception, pregnancy, childbirth and the early weeks of motherhood are profoundly significant life stages for most women and, indeed, for fathers as well. This book focuses on baptism - our new birth into Christ's risen life - but it is also appropriate to take a few moments to consider liturgical provision for the events that surround childbirth, since many of those who come to us for baptism come along with their newly born infants.

The development of the liturgical provision

The Book of Common Prayer

B4 ➤ The service commonly called The Churching of Women ➤ has gained a poor reputation among contemporary women. It is viewed as an imposed purification of a woman, a liturgy to signify a return to 'cleanness' after the messiness of birth and its aftermath. The proper title of the service, The Thanksgiving of Women after Childbirth, gives a much clearer indication of its true purpose.

Childbirth in the United Kingdom in the twenty-first century is not the potential death sentence that it was in the sixteenth and seventeenth centuries, but it continues to be risky. Women often face complications and some do die in labour. Thanksgiving for the safe passage of the mother through the ordeal is no less appropriate than for the miracle of creation and the birth of a wonderful baby.

The Book of Common Prayer service, is a short, affirming, mother-centred liturgy in which all concerned give thanks to God for her safe delivery through childbirth, and there is no mention of the child at all. There is no liturgy quite like this anywhere else in authorized Anglican provision.

Alternative Service Book and *Common Worship*

The revision of Anglican services that began in the latter half of the twentieth century moved through Thanksgiving for the Birth of a Child/for Adoption (*Alternative Service Book*) to Thanksgiving for the Gift of a Child (*Common Worship*), ➤ which is essentially a child-centred liturgy, with a prayer or two for the parents in the task ahead. It is interesting to note that thanksgiving for the mother's safe passage through labour has been lost altogether, except in an optional prayer for use after a difficult birth.

➤**D2**

Rites on the Way

The new Rites on the Way provision in *CW Christian Initiation* are for those who are approaching baptism. They are deliberately linked with Christian initiation, rather than with childbirth. Prayers surrounding conception, pregnancy, the approach of birth, difficulties during labour and miscarriage have been left, on the whole, to hospital chaplains and the slow accumulation of independent books of prayers and liturgy.

The original draft of the Rites on the Way material, published as a General Synod miscellaneous document for July 1998 included a selection of prayers for use before and after childbirth. Some were gleaned from material already in the public domain, in prayer and service books from the provinces of New Zealand, Australia, the USA, for example; many (including those printed below) were written by Michael Vasey, who died before that General Synod meeting took place. He drafted 'Towards an Introduction' for this selection, providing the rationale for including such prayers and rites in the book, and indicating an important distinction between them and baptism.

[*Rites on the Way*, GS Misc 530]

[*Rites on the Way*, page 27]

> 'The reception of a child into the human community is an important moment. It is appropriate both for the child, the parents and for the community that it should be marked in significant ways. The creation of a new human being within the relationship of two people is a wonder of creation. However baptism is not a birth rite but the application to an individual of the life-changing coming of Jesus Christ into the world . . . The forms of service that follow are not replacements for baptism; they are intended to enable families to bring the mystery of their life into the presence of God and to enable them, where they so wish, to grow into the new reality God has made known to us in Jesus Christ and declares to us in the sacrament of baptism.'

So having some of this material available, as well as the Thanksgiving for the Gift of a Child, may help us to meet the needs of those who might come to us thinking to use the Baptism service simply as a birth rite, and at the same time help them to relate to God about what is happening to them.

Prayers surrounding childbirth

See also Richard Deadman, Jeremy Fletcher, Janet Hudson, Stephen Oliver (eds), *Pastoral Prayers*, Mowbray, 1996, pages 16–26.

The prayers that follow give something of the flavour of this approach, and will be of value to those who are looking for such material when ministering to women, couples and families who have certain needs when they bring a child or children for baptism

Prayer for conception

Faithful God,
you heard Hannah and Elkanah, Elizabeth and Zechariah,
when they prayed for the child for whom they longed,
and gave them joy in their grief and despair;
look with kindness on this couple,
free them from fear and despair,
grant them the desire of their heart
and set their hope on your kingdom that will last for ever.
Amen.

Blessing of a couple expecting a child

Blessed are you, sovereign God,
source of love, giver of life.
Look in mercy on *this couple/N and N*;
protect the life that you have entrusted to them;
give them joy and faith as they walk together;
prepare them for all that lies ahead;
sharing in the mystery of your creation,
may they set their hearts on your kingdom
and forever praise you,
Father, Son and Holy Spirit.
Blessed be God for ever.

Blessing of a pregnant woman

O Lord and giver of life,
receive our prayer for *N* and for the child she carries,
that that they may happily come to the time of birth and,
serving you in all things
may rejoice in your loving providence.
We ask this through our Lord Jesus Christ,
who lives and reigns with you and the Holy Spirit,
one God, now and for ever.
Amen.

Prayer for a couple who cannot have children

Faithful God,
you are near to the broken-hearted
and give us in Jesus Christ
an inheritance that cannot be taken away;
may *this couple/N and N* know your consolation in their
suffering
and, through your resurrection power,
may their lives be made fruitful
and their longings be fulfilled in your kingdom of life;
through Jesus Christ our Lord.
Amen.

Prayers with a mother after the birth of a child

Blessed are you, Sovereign God, who gives us life;
you carry us in your arms as your children;
you lead us with cords of love;
you reach down and feed us.
When we turned away to darkness and chaos,
like a mother you would not forsake us.
You cried out like a woman in labour
and rejoiced to bring forth a new people.
In your Son you delivered us from darkness
to the gentle rule of your love.
Blessed are you, Sovereign God, who gives us life.
Blessed be God for ever.

A prayer of thanksgiving

Loving and gracious God,
we praise you that you have brought *N*
safely through the pain and danger of childbirth.
Be with her in the days and years ahead.
Restore her body and fill her with joy and faith.
Grant her wisdom and strength as a mother.
Give her freedom and confidence
to take her place again in the community of your people;
through Jesus Christ our Lord.
Amen.

This prayer could be appropriate at many Thanksgiving services.

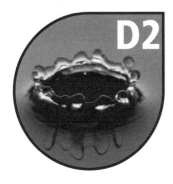

Thanksgiving for the Gift of a Child

The success of a service of Thanksgiving for the Gift of a Child will depend not just on the words that are spoken, but on the mood and feel of the service, so that the congregation go home not just knowing about God's love for them and the child, but sensing it too.

B4 ⬥

The service is designed to be used flexibly and appropriately, and this section makes some suggestions for the minister taking the service about basic good practice, and how to use the flexibility to allow the liturgical practice to meet the pastoral need ⬥ as well as possible.

Making the most of the flexibility

The notes at the end of the service make clear that it should be adapted for particular pastoral requirements. This would include situations such as:

- when only one parent is present;
- when the service is a celebration of adoption, rather than birth;
- when the child is older, and the service is therefore more about celebrating the child's *presence*, rather than their recent *arrival*;
- when the service is part of a main Sunday service, rather than a special 'stand-alone' service;
- when the service is taking place in a home, rather than at church.

In addition, although the service provides forms of words for most sections, sometimes more informal words may be more appropriate, either in addition to, or instead of the printed text.

Thanksgivings as part of a Sunday service

Thanksgivings can take place as part of a main Sunday service, but do not have to do so. This is one of the choices to place before parents, and will make the biggest difference when planning the service.

For a Thanksgiving within a Eucharist, natural places to put the thanksgiving part would be in the Gathering section (which means the family can then relax and enjoy the rest of the service), or after the sermon and before the prayers of intercession. For a non-eucharistic service, the possibilities will be greater, but the equivalent parts of the service are the natural places to consider.

Time and venue

Though most Thanksgiving services are likely to take place in a church building and on a Sunday, this does not have to be the case. For those with complicated work patterns, or family travelling from great distances, Saturdays and even weekdays or evenings may be more suitable.

Similarly, while some will naturally expect the service to take place in the church building, the possibility of a service in the child's home should be raised, and may well feel the more natural solution for some families.

The orders of service, or the opening remarks by the minister, will need to address some of the questions that will be in the minds of the congregation:

- Where should we sit?
- Will there be a collection?
- Can I use my camera or camcorder?
- How long will the service last?
- Is this the same as 'christening'?

Dramatic moments

Because a Thanksgiving does not have the natural 'dramatic' moments that a baptism has (the application of water, making the sign of the cross on the child's forehead, moving to the font, giving of a lighted candle, and so on) it is tempting to import some of them. However, in the long term, making the sign of the cross on the child's forehead, giving candles to the child, and so on can cause great confusion between the two services, so such things are best avoided. Instead, look for the dramatic moments in the Thanksgiving service itself and make the most of them.

For instance:

- Get the congregation to stand for the blessing of the child; emphasize that it is important that they join in with the 'Amen'.

Which parts to include

The bare minimum to insert into a main service would be:

> The Thanksgiving and Blessing section
>
> The Giving of the Gospel section (including the pledge by the supporting friends)

The Introduction section may or may not be appropriate.

- Make something of the presentation of certificate and gospel book – a great opportunity to involve older siblings.
- Encourage generous applause as a sign of love and support for the child after the presentation of certificate and gospel.
- Sign the Thanksgiving register in the sight of the congregation, tell them what you are doing, and invite them to come and inspect the entry afterwards.

Step by step through the service

The Introduction

The printed introductory words set the service in a wider perspective and can be used as printed, or as a pattern for similar or more informal words to mark the beginning of the service.

The responses

These are optional, and pick up the connections between this child and Jesus' human experience of being born and growing up.

Bible reading and sermon

Starting point for a brief sermon

Jesus' words about 'receiving the kingdom of God like a child' make a good way into talking about what it is to be a Christian, how Jesus turns our expectations upside down, and how children have much to teach as well as to learn.

The obvious reading in most cases will be the passage about Jesus blessing the children (Mark 10.13-16 and the parallel passages in Luke and Matthew). This gives a natural starting point for explaining where this service comes from, and for affirming God's delight in children. Other suggestions are given on page 23 of *CW Christian Initiation*. In most situations a short 'thought' will be more appropriate than a formal sermon.

Because a separate service of thanksgiving is geared to the needs of a particular family, it is a great opportunity for family and friends to contribute, perhaps by doing the Bible reading or reading out a poem or other piece of writing which is special to them. Good places to include such elements are either here or before the prayers.

Thanksgiving and Blessing

This is the point at which the parents and supporting friends bring the child to the front. An informal presentation of the child to the congregation will be a natural way to handle this.

The two opening questions establish why we are here, and lead naturally into the prayer of thanksgiving that follows.

Asking the child's name

The growth in popularity of secular (or even 'new age') naming ceremonies is a sign of how important a ritual naming still is to many people. Instead of the formal question in the service 'What name have you given this child?' it can be handled more informally, perhaps with a question about why the parents have chosen the name - though you'll need to warn them beforehand. ➤

➤B4

Blessing the child

The inclusion of a formal blessing of the child recognizes that 'having a child blessed' is often the way that parents articulate their desire for God to do something for their child.

The 'blessing' is phrased in such a way as to allow for a minister who is not a priest (such as a lay reader or a deacon) to use it as printed:

> As Jesus took children in his arms and blessed them, so now we ask God's blessing on *N*.
>
> Heavenly Father, we praise you for *his/her* birth;
> surround *him/her* with your blessing
> that *he/she* may know your love,
> be protected from evil,
> and know your goodness all *his/her* days.

It will be natural for the minister to take an infant into his or her arms for the blessing, laying a hand gently on the child's head. However, sometimes this causes nothing but distress for the child (and the parents) and it is better to let a parent hold the child.

For older children, a hand laid on the shoulder is often a good way to pray for them, especially if the minister kneels down to come to the child's level. Siblings and parents can be involved by inviting them to lay a hand on the child's shoulder during the prayer. Older children will benefit from having this explained to them in advance of the service.

The congregational prayer that follows makes clear that this service is not a baptism, and naturally prays that, in due time, baptism (and faith in Christ) will follow. As phrased in *CW Christian Initiation*, it works well when there are several children. If there is only one child, the 'they' can trip the congregation up, as they have to mentally change it to 'he' or 'she'. If your thanksgiving services are normally for one child, it would be best to produce your own order of service and make things simpler by printing the prayer as 'May this child learn to love all that is true . . .', which works for both boys and girls.

May they learn to love all
   that is true,
grow in wisdom and strength
and, in due time, come
   through faith and baptism
to the fullness of your grace;
through Jesus Christ our
   Lord.
Amen.

CWCI, page 20

Blessing the parents

Parents often speak of the huge sense of responsibility they feel at the arrival of a child, and the prayer of blessing for them is a wonderful way of helping them to *feel* supported by God and the church, as well as *asking for* his aid in the task of parenthood. The notes suggest the inclusion of the parents' names in the prayer. It may be appropriate to invite them to kneel (perhaps at the chancel step) for the prayer.

Giving of the Gospel

This is another section in which a more informal approach may be more natural. The inside cover of the Gospel can be inscribed with the child's name and the date of the service, and parents encouraged to keep the book with the child's other special things until they are old enough to have it read to them or can read it for themselves.

If a certificate is also to be presented at this point (especially if it includes the names of the supporting friends), then it may make sense to ask the questions of supporting friends and congregation first, and then to present Gospel and certificate together.

A Thanksgiving certificate

At the time of writing there are a few commercially available certificates and no registers for Thanksgiving services. Parishes will therefore need to produce their own.

Here are two possible sets of wording for a certificate:

Church Name

On [date of service]

public thanks was given to Almighty God, Father, Son and Holy Spirit, for the precious gift of [name of child]

who was born on [date of birth].

Parents: [name/s]

Supporting Friends: [names]

Minister: [name]

[Child's name] was brought to [Church Name]

on [date]

to be blessed by God in a service of Thanksgiving for the Gift of a Child.

Signed: [Minister's name]

Those acting as supporting friends were: [names]

A suitable Bible passage, or prayer from the service could also be included.

Prayers

The congregational prayer at the top of page 21 in *CW Christian Initiation* can also trip up a congregation as they mentally adjust for *them, him* or *her*. In a locally produced order of service, a simple adjustment to the wording of the prayer can avoid the problem:

> God our creator,
> we thank you for the gift of this child,
> entrusted to our care.
> May we be patient and understanding,
> ready to guide and to forgive,
> so that our love may be a sign of your love;
> through Jesus Christ our Lord.
> **Amen.**

CW Christian Initiation gives a selection of additional prayers on pages 24–7. As prayer forms a large part of the whole service, further prayers at this stage are probably best kept short and simple.

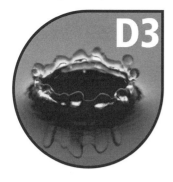

D3 Baptism service structure

Baptism symbolizes the transition from an old life to a new life in Christ and the structure of the Baptism service mirrors this. This transition is mirrored in the Baptism service itself. The administration of the water is at the centre. Before it there is teaching and a formal expression of commitment to discipleship. After come commissioning, prayer and sending out to do Christ's will. The pattern of the journey is the same for adults and children, as the Commentary makes clear:

[*CWCI*, page 333]

> 'For both . . . the service has the same inner logic, a movement from welcome and renunciation through to an identification with the people of God in their dependence on God, their profession of the saving name, and the common activities of prayer, eucharist and mission.'

The aim of this chapter is to set out clearly the detailed structure of the Baptism service in *Common Worship*, and to distinguish the following:

- the main mandatory sections (in the main column, against the left-hand margin) from
- the parts that are optional (in the main column, but indented).

In this chapter the different elements of the *CW Christian Initiation* service of Holy Baptism are denoted as follows:

It is important to distinguish between

- **Thanksgiving Prayer for a Child** (page 166) – a single prayer giving thanks for the gift of new life, used early in the Baptism service.
- **Thanksgiving for the Gift of a Child** (page 16) – a complete thanksgiving service which may be used on its own or as part of Sunday worship. [B4, D2]
- **Thanksgiving for Holy Baptism** (page 184) – usually part of Morning or Evening Prayer, helping the regular congregation focus on baptism.

¶ **Titles of the main sections**
Parts of the service sections
Elements within those parts

The outside margin has notes to guide you, some of which are taken from *CW Christian Initiation*: from the rubrics (set in *italics*), the notes to the service, or the Commentary at the end of the book.

¶ **Preparation**

Hymn

The Greeting

Words of welcome or introduction

Thanksgiving Prayer on page 166; note the accompanying rubric on that page

Introduction

Gloria in excelsis

Other words may be used. Seasonal introductions are on pages 150–66.

The Collect

Silent prayer precedes the saying of the appropriate Collect

The Collect of the Day or a seasonal collect may be used (pages 150–65)

¶ The Liturgy of the Word

'The Liturgy of the Word and the sermon are an opportunity to set the story of what God has done in Christ alongside our own story – to explore both the points of convergence and of difference.'

Readings

Page 6

On Sundays and Festivals the readings of the day are normally used. For seasonal readings, see pages 150–65, 167.

Either one or two readings may precede the Gospel.

Psalmody, canticles, hymns and songs may be used between the readings.

'Whenever Holy Baptism is administered there shall be a sermon.'

Note 2, page 98.

Gospel Reading

Sermon

'The presentation of the candidates and their welcome by the congregation acknowledges a shared responsibility for their growth in faith and flows naturally into a solemn renunciation of evil and the expression of the desire to follow Christ. At this stage, the candidates are identified with the believing community and reminded of the cost of discipleship by receiving the sign of the cross, the badge of the pilgrim community on the journey of faith.'

¶ The Liturgy of Baptism

Presentation of the Candidates

The candidates may be presented to the congregation. Where appropriate, they may be presented by their godparents or sponsors.

Introduction, page 6

The presentation of the candidates may also take place between the Introduction and the Collect.

Question to candidates who are able to answer for themselves.

Testimony by the candidate(s).

Children old enough to speak may answer with their parents and godparents (Note 6, page 99). Families baptized together answer 'We reject . . .'

The president addresses the congregation: 'Faith is the gift of God . . .'

At the baptism of children two sets of questions are put to the parents and godparents.

The Alternative Form of the Decision on page 168 may be used.

The Decision

A large candle may be lit.

Triple renunciation of the devil and evil by the candidates or on behalf of the candidates by parents and godparents.

Triple profession of adherence to Christ.

The signing comes either here or after the baptism. The two positions have different purposes. When used before baptism it signifies Christ's claim upon those who have just committed themselves to him as their Saviour and Lord. They are encouraged to persist in this new faith:
'Do not to be ashamed to confess the faith of Christ crucified.'

Signing with the Cross

When used after baptism it signifies the continuing of the journey for one born of water and the Spirit as we pray for the continual pouring out of God's grace and the daily renewing of his Spirit. As Christ is the anointed one so this candidate is anointed in his name.

See pages 169–76 for canticles and a couple of litanies for singing 'in Procession to the Font'.

Seasonal and responsive forms of the prayer over the water may be used (pages 150–65, 177). In their different ways these enhance the symbolism and also give opportunity for greater congregational participation.

Oil may be used (Note 10, page 100)

The president or another minister makes the sign of the cross.

The president may invite parents, sponsors and godparents to sign candidates with the cross.

Prayer over the Water

Ministers and candidates gather at the font.

A canticle, psalm, hymn or litany may be used.

The president says the prayer over the water.

'In this pilgrim faith, the community journeys to the font. The candidates express their longing for the transforming grace of God's Holy Spirit in the Prayer over the Water, and identify with the community's profession of faith as they say the Creed together.'

Introduction, page 7

Profession of Faith

Triple profession of faith, using the Apostles' Creed.

An Alternative Profession of Faith may be used (page 178).

Baptism

Question to candidate(s) able to answer for themselves.

The president or another minister dips each candidate in water, or pours water on them, saying *N*, I baptize you

> Clothing with a white robe.
>
> *Hymn or song*
>
> Signing with the cross (if not done after the Decision).

Prayer: 'May God, who has received you by baptism . . .'

> *The oil of chrism may be used if the signing with the cross comes at this point (Note 10, page 100).*
>
> Giving of lighted candle, if not to be given at end of service (Note 17, page 101).

Commission

Either: Form for those unable to answer for themselves.
Or: Form for those able to answer for themselves.

Prayers of Intercession

The Welcome and the Peace

Words of welcome.

> *The congregation may greet the newly baptized.*

The Peace

¶ The Liturgy of the Eucharist

'A triple administration of water is recommended; a single administration is lawful and valid. A substantial amount of water is desirable.'

Note 12, page 100

'Then, supported by the community, each candidate steps alone (or is carried) to the waters to be baptized in a lonely yet corporate embracing of Christ's dying and rising.'

Introduction, page 6

If the newly baptized person is clothed with a white robe, a hymn or song may be sung, and optional words are provided on page 71.

This form may be paraphrased or the contents included in the sermon (Note 15, page 101).

This form may be used at the Sending Out.

Either here or after the Welcome and Peace. Other forms or seasonal forms may be used (see pages 150–65, 179).

'The rationale for [including intercessions here] is that one of the responsibilities of the newly baptized within the Church is to take their proper place, as members of the royal priesthood, in the privilege and responsibility of public intercession.'

Commentary, page 337

If the signing is done at the later point, it should accompany the prayer, 'May God who has received . . .' and the words provided for the signing at the Decision should not be used (Note 11, page 100).

If the lighted candle is given at the earlier point in the service, it either has to be held throughout the service, or (unhelpfully from a symbolic point of view) blown out straight away. An alternative might be to provide some simple stand for the candle to be placed in, beside the font, until it can be collected at the end of the service.

'What is the new life like? It is a life directed and empowered by the Spirit, who overshadowed Jesus as he came up from the waters of baptism. As candidates emerge from the waters, they may be clothed – putting on Christ – and anointed as a sign of their belonging with all the baptized in the royal priesthood of God's holy people. At this point in the service, they may hear a commission or charge to live out the baptized life. They then take their place in the Church through participation in the prayers of intercession and in the action of the Eucharist.'

Introduction, page 7

Seasonal forms or another suitable blessing may be used (pages 150–65).

The candle(s) may be lit from the large candle lit at the decision. The candle may be given immediately after baptism (Note 17, page 101).

At the end of the service, the commission may be used if it has not been heard earlier and the newly baptized are sent out with a lighted candle, as a sign of the Church's commitment to mission: 'Shine as a light in the world to the glory of God the Father.'

¶ The Sending Out

Commission to those able to answer for themselves – if not used earlier.

The Blessing

Giving of a Lighted Candle

The Dismissal

Longest and shortest?

The longest possible baptism service is probably two or three hours, maybe longer if it includes the renewal of baptism vows in the sea and a picnic. It could be an annual celebration of all that baptism means to the congregation, and involve, as well as the renewal of vows, some substantial teaching (not necessarily the traditional sermon), time for testimony and prayer ministry, an extended Peace and perhaps a celebration meal together after the Eucharist.

For the shortest, look down the left side of the main column only and omit all the optional material. Then examine the rubrics and marginal notes to see where (a) other, shorter options can be used (the Alternative Decision and Profession of Faith, for example) and (b) you can use your own words rather than the printed text (the Greeting, the words of the Commission and the prayers that follow are optional: see Note 15 on page 101, which also says you can include the Commission in the sermon). There are helpful notes on pages 78-9 on how to abbreviate the service to combine with the main Sunday Communion service. Note particularly that when baptism takes place in a Eucharist, the prayers of penitence and the creed are omitted.

Neither option should be pursued on every occasion!

Questions for discussion

1. What are the advantages and disadvantages of the two alternative positions for the signing with the cross?

2. How might we want to modify the words of the Commission to make them particularly appropriate for our locality?

Seasonal alternatives

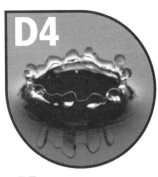

There is such a wealth of biblical and theological material about baptism that it is impossible to get it all into one service. ➤ The standard order of Holy Baptism in *Common Worship* is complete in itself, but - deliberately - does not say all that could be said. So other ways of speaking about baptism, other themes and biblical references, have been incorporated into sets of seasonal alternatives. The Church in the West has traditionally associated baptism with Easter, but in other traditions it has been linked with Epiphany or the Baptism of Christ, and with All Saints' tide. The alternatives for these seasons provide a different theological emphasis that is particularly suitable for that time of year. But they are not all tied to the season. The texts 'may be used on any occasion to meet pastoral circumstances.' Some churches might prefer, for instance, to use the Easter season material with its concentration on Christ's death and resurrection for all their baptism services throughout the year, and that is perfectly permissible.

➤ **D5**

[*CWCI*, page 150].

If the baptism takes place in the normal Sunday service, the readings for the day are used. But if there is a service where the principal focus is baptism, whether that is a small afternoon occasion or a major celebration with several baptisms, some seasonal sets of readings and psalms are provided. These can be used to complement the seasonal texts and bring out their themes and, like the seasonal texts, are not confined to any point of the church year.

They are not intended to replace the Sunday readings - not only might they become stale for the Sunday congregation, but there is a risk of losing the thread of semi-continuous readings in the lectionary.

Each of the three seasonal patterns provides not only a full set of alternative texts and readings for both baptism and confirmation, but also a suggested timetable for preparation, using the Rites on the Way material, that culminates with baptism at the particular festival.➤

➤ **C1 - C3**

> 'Rites on the Way support a journey of faith which in some ways mirrors the story of Jesus as it is told by the Christian community through the seasons. It is therefore appropriate to use the seasons to enhance the sense of journey and of the climax to that journey which is already firmly within the historical understanding of the faith.'
>
> Commentary, *CWCI*, page 330

What are the seasonal emphases?

Father, we give you thanks
   and praise
for your gift of water in
   creation;
for your Spirit, sweeping over
   the waters,
bringing light and life;
for your Son Jesus Christ our
   Lord,
baptized in the river Jordan.

Prayer over the Water, Epiphany, page 152

We thank you that through
   the waters of the Red Sea
you led your people out of
   slavery
to freedom in the Promised
   Land.
We thank you that through
   the deep waters of death
you brought your Son,
and raised him to life in
   triumph.

Prayer over the Water, Easter/Pentecost,
page 158

Lord of the heavens,
we bless your name for all
   your servants
who have been a sign of your
   grace through the ages.
You delivered Noah from the
   waters of destruction;
you divided the waters of the
   sea,
and by the hand of Moses
you led your people from
   slavery
into the Promised Land.

Prayer over the Water, All Saints, page
163

Epiphany

Epiphany and the Baptism of Christ, both early in January, are natural occasions for baptism, and references to birth link naturally into the preceding Christmas season. This set of material recalls Jesus' baptism, but as the Bible accounts bring together the work of God the Father, God the Son and God the Holy Spirit, this set of texts is also particularly suitable for use at Trinity. Apart from references to Jesus' baptism, some of the key words in this seasonal set are:

- rebirth
- new birth
- new creation.

Easter

In the early church Easter was *the* time for baptism, and candidates were prepared through Lent. Easter itself, the great celebration of Christ's dying and rising again, was the occasion for candidates to share in that dying and rising through baptism. The images in the material are of death and resurrection, of going from slavery through water into freedom, of being united with Christ. Key concepts include:

- dying to sin
- rising to new life
- life in the Spirit.

All Saints

Baptism is also a symbol of becoming part of Christ's Church, and joining the community of all believers. A baptism around the festival of All Saints would naturally bring out this emphasis, and the seasonal material is provided for that purpose. Some of the key terms and emphases used in this season include:

- the company of the faithful
- the covenant of grace
- being fellow-citizens
- the household of God.

Questions for discussion

1. Could we make more use of the seasonal alternatives in our pattern of initiation services?

2. Would any of the seasonal sets, with their particular emphases, be useful at other times in our situation?

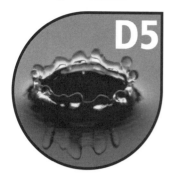

D5

Use of the Bible

The initiation services are packed full with a multitude of biblical themes and images: redemption and rescue, salvation from sin, repentance and discipleship, grace and faith, creation and the cross, death and life, birth and new birth, witness and welcome – the list could go on. These great motifs, which lie at the heart of the services also, of course, dominate the pages of Scripture.

The aim of this section is to help people explore the enormous wealth of biblical material available in relation to baptism, so that good choices can be made of themes and passages appropriate to each situation

The theological argument in the Commentary (pages 319-22) is profoundly biblical and traces the journey of the initiate through four stages:

- **Separation** from a sinful world that is estranged from God. This leave-taking is not necessarily in the strength of the initiate, but as a result of God's intervention.
- **Reception** into the new community centred on God, with all the new relationships and disciplines that entails.
- **Growth** into the pattern of Christ, so that in the long term a gradual increase in holiness, knowledge, wisdom and strength may be discerned. ➤

E2, E3 ➤

E4 ➤
- **Mission** –involvement in God's plan for humanity, so that other individuals, and society at large, can be transformed also. ➤

Themed readings for baptism and confirmation

Where to find

The Index of Biblical References on pages 362ff of *CW Christian Initiation* shows where in the services the various scriptures are read. Alternatively, type the reference into *Visual Liturgy* to see where it it used.

The table on the following two pages combines the table on page 323 of *CW Christian Initiation* with most of the suggested readings for baptism and confirmation on page 167, and other material, grouping the passages into themes. It may be a resource to consult when choosing readings for a service, or to provide biblical references for use during the preparation of participants. And like the table on page 323 it can provide more than enough material for a long teaching course or series of sermons on baptism.

Even this is not an exhaustive list of initiation-related texts. One may find that the lectionary passage for any Sunday has a satisfactory link to an initiation theme – indeed we are encouraged to stay with the lectionary readings, especially from Advent to the Presentation, and from Ash Wednesday to Trinity Sunday. See also the seasonal tables on pages 151, 157, 162.

[*CWCI*, page 99, Note 5]

liberation	rescue from sin and flood	Genesis 6–8
and rescue	freedom from slavery in Egypt	Exodus 3.7-12
	safe from earthquake and war	Psalm 46
	he preserves our lives	Psalm 66.4-12
	through water and fire unscathed	Isaiah 43.1-7
	freedom from sin	Romans 6.22-23 and
		Revelation 1.5
	rescue from darkness	Colossians 1.13
	the ark and baptism	1 Peter 3.18-22
covenant	with Abraham	Genesis 17.1-11, 22.15-18
	with Moses	Exodus 19.3-6
	heirs of Abraham through Christ	Galatians 3.16-29
new creation	new creation	Galatians 6.15
		2 Corinthians 5.17
		Isaiah 51.9-11
	liberation from Babylon as a new exodus,	Genesis 1.2
	defeating the dragon of chaos	
new birth	'born again'	John 3.1-8 and
		1 Peter 1.3,23
	birth through the word	James 1.18
response to the Gospel	the hearers of John the Baptist	Mark 1.1-5
	the Ethiopian eunuch	Acts 8.26-39
	baptism follows Peter's preaching to Cornelius' household	Acts 10.34-48
reconciliation	no longer enemies	Romans 5.6-11
	not counting our sins	2 Corinthians 5.18 - 6.2
grace of God	undeserved love from God	Ephesians 2.1-10 and
		Titus 3.3-7
illumination	God, the maker of light	Genesis 1.3
	we are light for the world	Matthew 5.14-16
	light and truth	John 3.16-21
	the blind will see	John 9
	the armour of light	Romans 13.11-14
	God's light in our hearts	2 Corinthians 4.4-6
	enlightenment	Ephesians 1.18 and
		Hebrews 6.4-6
	called into his light	1 Peter 2.9-10
recognition	receiving the name of Christ	James 2.7 and
		Isaiah 43.1
water of life	water flowing from the temple	Ezekiel 47
	Jesus and the Samaritan woman	John 4.1-15
	Jesus the water of life	John 7.37-41

cleansing	Naaman washes in the Jordan	2 Kings 5.1-15a
	'Cleanse me with hyssop'	Psalm 51.1-7
	'I will sprinkle clean water'	Ezekiel 36.24-28
	Peter and the washing of feet	John 13.3-14
	removal of defilement	Romans 3.25
	washed, sanctified and justified	1 Corinthians 6.11
	washed like a bride	Ephesians 5.26
	the washing of rebirth	Titus 3.5
	sprinkled clean	Hebrews 10.22
	atoning sacrifice	1 John 2.2; 4.10
stripping	putting off the old human	Colossians 3.9
	the Christian analogue to circumcision	Colossians 2.11
clothing	putting on Christ	Galatians 3.27
	the new human	Colossians 3.10
dying	the ordeal foreshadowed in his own baptism	Mark 10.38 and Luke 12.50
	Participation in Christ's 'exodus' drowning, burial	Luke 9.31 Romans 6.3ff and Colossians 2.11-12
resurrection	dry bones can live	Ezekiel 37.1-14
	new life, new hope, new role	John 21.1-17
	into newness of life	Romans 6.3ff and Colossians 2.12; 3.1ff
united with Christ	united in death and resurrection	Romans 6.5
	new life in our mortal bodies	Romans 8.11
	we belong to the Lord	Romans 14.7ff
	the life of Jesus revealed in us	2 Corinthians 4.10
	Christ lives in me	Galatians 2.20
	Christ will be exalted in my body	Philippians 1.20
the new community	the fruitful vine	John 15.1-8
	children of God	Romans 8.12-21 and Galatians 4.1-7
	as living stones in a new temple	1 Corinthians 3.9-17 and Ephesians 2.19-21 and 1 Peter 2.4ff
	all baptized into one body	1 Corinthians 12.4-13
disciples	tasked with making *new* disciples	Matthew 28.16-20
	the cost of following	Mark 8.31-38
	forsaking family	Luke 9.57-62
	life of the earliest church	Acts 2.37-47
	fight the good fight	1 Timothy 6.11-16
	disciplined children of God	Hebrews 12.1-11
	made priests to serve our God	Revelation 5.9-10
pilgrim people	the Israelites crossing the sea	Exodus 13.17-22
	Israelites baptized into Moses	1 Corinthians 10.1-4
	looking for the city to come	Hebrews 13.8-14
	heading towards the heavenly city	Revelation 22.1-5

Presentation

When using any of the texts in this table as a reading in an initiation service, those planning the service should check its suitability in the church's preferred translation, and consider whether to modify its length. Consideration also needs to be given to how best to present the text in a lively way - especially if there are guests in church who are not used to listening to the Bible.

- If the text is a narration with some dialogue, can different **voices** be used to reflect this? You may think it worth doing some re-writing to take advantage of the extra clarity that this approach can give.
- Can you go as far as to **dramatize** the passage?
- Could the narrative be **re-told** from the point of view of one of the characters in the story?
- Could **music** be used as a background to the reading, or to punctuate it? Could the text even be set to music?
- Can suitable **images** be projected behind the reader?
- Could a short text be read by the whole **congregation** together?

Any of these methods has the potential to communicate the Scripture message to a deeper level in the minds of the congregation.

Could Scripture be presented in an imaginative way also in the context of the preparation group? Will those being prepared be asked to read passages at home? Can you rely on their having Bibles at home, and being able to navigate through them? Or do you need to provide the text on paper or electronic media? Will you ask people to learn passages by heart? The Four Texts are obvious candidates for this, but there are also others worth learning.

Thanksgiving for the Gift of a Child

The Bible readings for the service of Thanksgiving for the Gift or a Child on page 23 of *CW Christian Initiation* are included here, along with some others, with some indication of their theological theme.

God the creator and author of life		Genesis 1
The first born of all creation		Colossians 1.15-20
The gift of children, the grace of God	Moses	Exodus 2.1-10
	Hannah , Elkanah and Samuel	1 Samuel 1
God's antenatal love	you knit me together in my mother's womb	Psalm 139.7-18
	The child in my womb leaped for joy	Luke 1.39-45
God's blessings	The Lord bless you and keep you	Numbers 6.22-27
	May he grant you your heart's desire	Psalm 20
	May you see your children's children	Psalm 128
	Filled with all the fullness of God	Ephesians 3.14-21
God who calls his lost children to return	The Father of the lost son	Luke 15.11-32
	God's call is merciful and effective	Isaiah 55.6-11
The Incarnation	A child born for us	Isaiah 9.2,6,7
	The birth of Jesus	Matthew 1.18-25
	Jesus presented in the Temple	Luke 2.22-40
	He gave power to become children of God	John 1.9-14
Jesus' attitude to children	Whoever welcomes one ... in my name welcomes me	Matthew 18:1-5
	Whoever does not receive the kingdom of God as a little child ...	Mark 10.13-16
	Do not despise one of these little ones	Matthew 18.10-14
Family relationships	Honour your father and mother	Exodus 20.12
	Spiritual education	Deuteronomy 6.20-25
	Obedience and education	Ephesians 6.1-4
	Family strengths and weaknesses	1 John 2.12-14

Confirmation, Affirmation and Reception

The tables on pages 151, 157, 162 and 167 of *CW Christian Initiation* offer readings for use at a confirmation, for confirmation when there is also an affirmation of baptismal faith and/or a reception into the Communion of the Church of England, and short readings which come in the earlier part of the vigil when baptism and confirmation take place then.

Use of testimonies

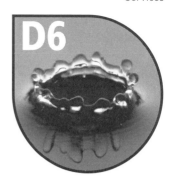

D6

Giving the candidates a chance to share their stories has a number of benefits:

- the regular congregation learn more about those who are being added to their number, and will better understand them, and so be able to help them grow;
- guests with less understanding of the Christian faith will hear how God touches and changes the lives of people like them;
- the candidates themselves gain a deeper understanding of their own story, and how to tell it – and having told it in public will be more confident telling it in other situations.

Those planning the service may choose how many of the candidates to ask to speak in this way. It might be right to ask all the candidates at a particular service to do so.

However it is important to plan and prepare ahead of time. 'Telling your own story', whether live or on paper, might be an exercise in one of the later preparation classes. Having shared with the rest of the group, the course leader could tell the group that some (at least) of these unique personal accounts will encourage others if shared at the Baptism service.

Speak, write, or show?

A candidate who stands in front of a congregation, and tells their story, even with limited eloquence, makes a strong impact.

Some churches like to print the stories of most or all of the candidates – either in the service booklet, or in a separate leaflet to take away. The advantages of this are that the candidates have time to prepare their texts in advance, and the congregation can mull over the experiences recounted at their leisure, when they've got home. At a confirmation, it may also help the bishop to refer to them in his sermon more easily.

A printed text can be enhanced by photos of the candidates. A printed testimony does not have to be restricted to simple narrative: candidates who are children may have produced artwork during the course of preparation which could be reproduced, and poetry and other creative writing can be a very powerful way of conveying the story of moving from darkness to light. However, the printed word lacks the immediacy of the spoken voice; and there may be

The rubrics provide for testimony not only in the services of Holy Baptism (*CWCI*, page 66) and confirmation (page 111) but also in the Celebration after an Initiation Service outside the parish (page 183), Thanksgiving for Holy Baptism (page 185) and the Affirmation of Baptismal Faith (page 200). So both reflection on the event and a desire to say something about personal renewal may give rise to testimony. And testimony is also encouraged in the preliminary Rites on the Way:

'The giving of a personal testimony in these rites or in an initiation service is to be encouraged. It is a public opportunity both for the new disciples to express their faith and for the Christian community to be encouraged and enthused to continue to spread the good news of God's kingdom. Such testimony will affirm the mission of the Church and allow the congregation to learn from the experience of the new disciples.'

Note 2, *CWCI*, page 30

Candidate photo options:

passport style
at home
at work
at leisure

elements of the story that the candidate is happy to share in the intimacy of worship service, but would not like to see circulating around the neighbourhood in print.

A third possibility, for venues where video technology is part of normal life, is to make a short video documentary, showing the candidate in significant settings.

A fourth approach is to prepare a display, telling the story in words and pictures, that people can look at during the refreshments after the service. It might be appropriate to leave this in place for a couple of weeks, for the benefit of others visiting the venue.

Structuring the story

An interview format often works well. An able interviewer can keep the candidate to the point, and make sure that obscure abbreviations or local references are made clear for guests. In addition, a dialogue can hold the attention of the listeners better than a monologue.

See *New Patterns for Worship,* page 30

Typical questions for an 'interview-style' testimony

- How long have you lived in...?
- What brings you to baptism now?
- How has your faith changed your life?
- What would you like us to pray for?

If the candidate is going to tell their story 'off the cuff', it is worth priming them with some key questions, and checking beforehand roughly what they are going to say. If they want to work from notes, or a written text, that's fine. Even though reading out a written text can sound somewhat wooden, the message is more important than style.

Obviously a story that is going to be presented in print can be edited and revised until both minister and candidate are happy with it.

Pitfalls

You can have **too much** of a good thing - although testimonies can be exciting and encouraging, you want to keep the service moving. Two or three short testimonies are probably enough. If you have a number of candidates then pick a couple which illustrate their variety: young and old, male and female, slow and quick conversion. So that the others do not feel left out, you could include all in a printed or notice board presentation.

Remember that we are all **fallible but saved**. Don't put the candidate on a high pedestal, or let her put herself on one - in case tomorrow she slips down from it. On the other hand, even the humblest candidate, who disclaims any virtue or worth, should be able to rejoice in some spiritual growth under God's grace.

Take care that the bounds of **privacy and decency** are not overstepped. For example:

- The candidate's story may be bound up with someone else's, which should not be made public: judgement needs to be exercised over revealing details and names, or permission should be sought from the other person where that is appropriate.
- The candidate's former way of life may have included some events which it may not be appropriate to describe in public.
- The candidate may be returning to a country where Christians are persecuted, or may have family members living in such a country; in this case printing the candidate's full name or photograph may invite unnecessary difficulties.

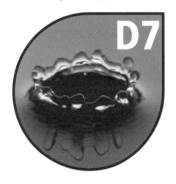

D7

Using symbolism well

One of the features of *Common Worship* is its emphasis on what we *do* in worship as well as what we *say*. In a culture that is increasingly visually stimulated rather than verbally stimulated, we are more and more aware of the power of symbols. It is the experience of many leaders of worship that people are far more likely to encounter God through what is done than through what is said, heard or sung.

For a very helpful guide to the symbolic possibilities in the baptism rites, see Gilly Myers *Using Common Worship: Initiation*, Church House Publishing, 2000, pages 39ff.

The *Common Worship* Baptism service mentions two sets of symbols: two that are mandatory and a few more that are optional. The wise use of these symbols can help make the service memorable to candidates and their families, and can maximize a sense of the presence of God, perceived not just through words but also beyond them.

How do symbols work?

A symbol is something that can speak other than through words to something other than the intellect. It is about 'deep calling to deep'.

- Symbols can reinforce words: to speak about anointing and to use oil can say the same thing in a different way.
- Symbols can subvert words: to speak about drowning and death in the presence of a candidate who is very much alive can demonstrate the paradox of Jesus' gift of new life.
- Symbols can blur and scatter words: they are by nature ambiguous and may mean different things to different people. They can allow different nuances to shine through. The symbol of water is extremely rich in its layers of meaning.
- Because of the ambiguity of symbols the Church has at times distrusted them and relied solely on words, in a quest for sound doctrine and accuracy. There is a tension between allowing symbols to speak to people in different ways, and yet making sure the service as a whole says what we want it to say. The use of symbols needs to go hand in hand with the Church's teaching ministry.

An excellent guide to worship beyond words alone is Peter Craig-Wild's *Tools for Transformation*, Darton, Longman & Todd, 2002.

- Compared with biblical descriptions of the use of symbol, the Church today is often very restrained. A teaspoon of water and a polite thumbprint of oil are very different from the gallons of water of the Feast of Tabernacles, the blood swilling around the altar from sacrifices and the oil running down the face onto the clothing! Without making too much of a slippery mess, we can probably afford to be a bit more extravagant in our use of symbol, thus illustrating the extravagant and outrageous grace of God.

Mandatory symbols: water and the sign of the cross

Water

This is *the* symbol of baptism. Whilst the language used of baptism has often been about washing or cleansing, it actually has more to do with drowning. The standard prayer over the water uses both these ideas:

> We thank you, Father, for the water of baptism.
> In it we are buried with Christ in his death.
> By it we share in his resurrection . . .
> Now sanctify this water that . . . they may be cleansed from sin.

This distinction is important: do we believe that sin is something from which we need cleansing, or is it such a radical problem that only dying and starting completely over again can deal with it? What does our symbolism imply? Can we be 'washed' from sin by a few drops of water on our heads, or do we need literally to go under and rise again? The increasing popularity of total immersion baptism, in spite of the inherent difficulties for Anglicans, whose buildings were not designed for adult submersion or immersion, shows a healthy understanding of the serious nature of sin and Jesus' radical solution for it.

How much water? ►   ►B10, D10

To make the symbol more extravagant, and to reinforce the idea of 'drowning' as opposed to 'washing', *Common Worship* encourages the use of 'a substantial amount of water': it 'must at least flow on the skin of the candidate'. In a church which is not equipped with a baptistery, it might be possible to

- use another building: a local or school swimming pool, or a non-conformist church;
- hire a birthing pool, a large paddling pool or a sheep dip, or club together as a deanery to buy one;
- go outdoors, to a local river or lake, or to the sea (recommended for summer months only!).

A threefold administration of water can be a symbolic reminder of the Trinity, although this is not strictly necessary.

Depending on the amount of water used, you will need to think about drying and/or changing afterwards. See below on 'Clothing'.

The sign of the cross

The signing of candidates with the cross is first mentioned by Tertullian at the end of the second century, and the idea grew in the medieval church that unless the sign was made the rites were ineffective. The Reformers rejected this 'superstitious' piece of doctrine, apart from Cranmer who allowed the sign to be used in baptism, as long as it was understood that it is merely a visual aid and not part of 'the substance of the sacrament'.

In spite of the Reformers' suspicion of the medieval practice of signing, it has remained an important symbol in Anglican baptism rites, although it has often been used in confused and confusing ways. The *Common Worship* service allows for signing in one of two places in the service. The two options, though, have different meanings, with different words to explain them. See section D10 for more detail about the two options.

Optional symbols: oil, candles, clothing, sprinkling and moving

[Commentary, *CWCI*, pages 343, 345ff]

Anointing with oil

Either of the two signings mentioned above may include the use of oil, but as with the two different meanings and texts, there is a difference of meaning in the oil too.

The 'oil of baptism' (or 'oil of exorcism') may accompany the prayer and signing before the Decision. As well as protection from the devil, this anointing may reflect the ancient practice of anointing athletes before they went out to compete. This particular piece of symbolism may not be immediately apparent to the congregation, and may need some explaining.

The 'oil of chrism' should accompany the signing if it takes place after the baptism. The symbolism here is twofold:

- the anointing with oil of those who, in the Old Testament, were taking on office as kings or priests, reflecting the entrance of the candidates into the royal priesthood of the Church;
- the anointing and equipping of the candidates with the gift of the Holy Spirit, empowering them with God's gifts for service in the Church.

Anointing is another example of a symbol whose use could be a little more extravagant!

Holy Oils

The bishop will normally bless three different types of oil at the Eucharist on Maundy Thursday.

- The Oil of Baptism, usually plain olive oil, is used before candidates are baptized with a prayer for deliverance and protection from the devil.
- The Oil of Chrism is scented and may be used as a sign of the Holy Spirit.
- The Oil for the Sick is used within the healing ministry. Stocks of the oils are normally kept in the cathedral for parishes to use.

Candles

Light is another powerful symbol with many nuances. The *Common Worship* rubrics suggest the use of 'a large candle' before the Decision, which might be lit by a candidate or a sponsor. The use of the Easter candle here would make a link with the death and resurrection of Christ, through which the candidates, symbolically, are about to follow.

From this large candle smaller ones may be lit and given to the candidates or their parents. *Common Worship* places this normatively at the end of the service, but allows an alternative position immediately after the baptism. See 'Journey' and 'Clashing symbols' below.

Remember too that there are other ways than candles of producing light. How about doing the first part of the service in semi-darkness, perhaps with words people need projected onto a screen, and then flooding the building with light at the point of baptism? Or how about a change of colour? For an evening service, how about using a couple of overhead projectors with coloured acetates rather than your 'house' lights?

Clothing

Common Worship provides for the ancient practice (still common in the Free Churches) of clothing candidates in white *after* the baptism rather than in preparation for it. This clothing might take the form of large white towels or dressing gowns for candidates who have been immersed, or some specially made and easy-to-get-into robes in which the candidates might be wrapped. The text picks up New Testament thought from texts such as Romans 13 and Colossians 3:

> 'You have been clothed with Christ . . .
> As many as are baptized into Christ have put on Christ.'

Ideally the clothing should happen immediately after the baptism, rather than after the candidates have disappeared and dressed again in their normal clothes. As long as they are not too wet and cold, they can get changed later, perhaps during a hymn or song. Babies being baptized could usefully be dressed in their 'christening robes' after the baptism, although there may be some parental resistance to this idea.

Sprinkling

On some occasions – even when a baptism is not taking place – particularly on Easter Eve, at the start of a new year or at the feast

E3→ of the Baptism of Christ, it will be appropriate for the whole congregation to renew their baptism promises (a text for this can be found in *CWCI*, pages 193-5). ● Of course, when a baptism *is* taking place, other Christians present are always reminded of their own baptism. In both cases the remembrance can be made more vivid by sprinkling them with water. There is no text for this, but the custom is for the sprinkling to happen with the words 'Remember your baptism into Christ'.

A proper 'aspergillum' (a brush or perforated ball for dispensing holy water) may be purchased from church suppliers, but a small branch (for instance, of conifer or rosemary) and a bowl of water work just as effectively. Those doing the sprinkling move among the congregation flicking the water over them with the twigs and using the words above.

The sprinkling is best done after the baptism and before the Commission, though alternative positions are possible.

Moving

An important feature of the *Common Worship* understanding of baptism is the idea of a journey. The spiritual journey of the individual to faith, the sense of the pilgrimage of the church community in their walk with God, with others joining in as they go, the journey outwards to the world in mission: all these may be reflected symbolically by allowing movement of the whole congregation, rather than just the baptismal party, during the service. Whether this takes the form of a solemn procession or a less organized scrum, to gather the congregation around the font for the baptism itself can speak of this sense of journey and movement. Obviously architecture will affect the ease with which movement can take place, but even turning the congregation to face the font at the rear is usually preferable to using a makeshift 'portable' font at the front.

We have already noted that the lighted candles are given to the candidates at the end of the service. This suggests the outward journey of the newly baptized, along with the rest of the congregation, to take the light of Christ out into a dark and needy world.

Clashing symbols

Because symbols can be so powerful, they need using with care. Three simple rules can mean that we use them effectively rather than counter-productively.

1. Make them say what you want to say

If you want to convey the extravagant generosity of God in pouring out his Holy Spirit, don't use oil as if it were rationed. If you believe that sin is more serious than a quick wash and brush-up, go for the drowning rather than the sprinkling symbolism. Let the symbols reinforce what you have said with words, perhaps during a sermon or talk, rather than contradict them.

2. Don't let them say what you don't want to say

The signing with the cross, whether you do it before or after the baptism itself, has, as we have seen, a distinct meaning, and is not a part of the actual baptism. To make the sign of the cross with water, rather than 'dry' or with oil, is to confuse the two unhelpfully. Similarly, if baptism candles are given immediately after baptism (rather than at the preferred point at the end of the service) there can be a clash of symbolism, as the light of Christ is symbolically given and then, unhelpfully, blown out almost straight away.

3. Don't try to say too much

An over-use of symbol can too easily suggest gimmick rather than powerful sign. You won't want to do everything suggested above in each and every baptism service. While there is much richness in the biblical images of death to sin and rebirth in Christ, we can only usefully expound a part of the story on each occasion.

Neither is it helpful, though, to make your church's practice into a stereotype by choosing a symbol or two for unvaried use. A better way is to let the baptism be flavoured by other factors, such as the season of the Church's year or a current teaching series. So during Lent you may want to focus on and use the symbols of light and darkness. During Advent your focus might be more on journeying towards the future. A Pentecost baptism might major on the anointing with the Holy Spirit and use oil more extravagantly. As you use the seasonal options in the text, you can choose which symbols to include accordingly.

For a fuller account of this subject see John Leach, *How to use symbol and action in worship,* Grove, 2005.

D8 Choosing appropriate music

The social diversity and liturgical developments described earlier in the book have profound implications for the church musician, who faces the challenge of choosing music which complements the initiation liturgy but which also fits the context and nature of the gathered congregation. Many of those who attend baptisms are not regular churchgoers, and are therefore unfamiliar even with hymns thought of as well known (and probably unused to singing at all).

It is important, then, that music is chosen which enables as many worshippers as possible to be included rather than alienated. This will mean careful thinking about the musical style most appropriate for a particular congregation: for some, Palestrina's *Sicut cervus* might just hit the spot; for others, Kendrick or Redman might be more appropriate.

At the heart of the drama

In any planning for worship, there is always the danger that music will be seen as an 'add-on' to the rest of the liturgy, rather than an integral part of it. Initiation liturgy is by nature highly dramatic. The promises to renounce evil and turn to Christ, the use of oil, light and water, and the symbolic dying and rising with Christ paint a vivid picture of baptism as a cataclysmic and life-changing sacrament. The music must enable this drama to shine through: the symbolism being reinforced by what is sung and played.

If initiation is celebrated within the Eucharist or a Service of the Word, those particular frameworks will inevitably dictate some of the musical content. However, even a stand-alone baptism benefits from a thoughtful use of music. Whereas the ASB allowed for a single hymn to be sung before the Prayer over the Water, the rubrics in *Common Worship* are peppered with references to music.

A clear understanding of the structure and flow of the liturgy is vital if musical choices are to make sense. Music must work with the liturgy and not against it. For instance, a prayerful hymn calling on the Holy Spirit (such as 'Come down, O love divine') might work well if sung while the candidates move to the font, or as the candidates gather at the place of confirmation, but misses its moment if sung later in the service. The *Common Worship* provision of three

[*CWCI*, pages 150ff.] **D4 ➜** streams of seasonal material ➜ gives an immediate way in to musical choices – not all of which necessarily have to relate to baptism or confirmation.

Music in the different sections of the service

The Preparation

At the start, a congregation needs to be gathered and the tone set with a familiar hymn or song. This need not be 'initiation-specific' but in seasonal time, might introduce a seasonal theme (a resurrection hymn in Eastertide, a 'kingdom' theme in the period before Advent), or at other times, could simply be a hymn or song of praise.

The Liturgy of the Word

Common Worship envisages a substantial Liturgy of the Word, which will need to include appropriate music. This is usually a good place to sing a shorter song or, possibly a version of one of the appointed psalms. If the gathered congregation is unused to singing, it is worth considering including a song sung by a worship group or choir at this point. Though a gradual hymn between readings is often assumed, sometimes a song or hymn after the sermon makes a useful opportunity for response. Again, this may be linked to baptism, or to the Bible reading(s), or simply a song or hymn of response to God.

The Liturgy of Baptism

- The movement of the candidate(s) to the baptismal font is a significant liturgical moment of journeying. Music at this point should aim to do much more than simply cover the footsteps. It should prepare the worshippers for what is about to happen.

- Some verses of a major hymn or song ('At the name of Jesus', 'Amazing Grace', 'Shine, Jesus, Shine', 'Great is the darkness' and others) can work well here. For a smaller gathering, a shorter, more gentle song (such as 'River, wash over me') might be more appropriate.

- There does not *have* to be congregational singing at this point. A piece from a choir (canticle or anthem) or worship band can work equally well here, as can an instrumental item.

- The Prayer over the Water is a wonderful piece of dramatic prose. The use of music during this prayer is to be encouraged. It could be an underlying musical current with presidential voice-over, or with sung responses (for seasonal and responsive forms of the prayer).

- *Common Worship* allows for a hymn or song to be sung if the newly baptized are to be clothed. The focus of this should be strongly on Christ.

- The return from the font can provide an opportunity for singing (perhaps the latter verses of the major hymn sung earlier), or can be just as effective with instrumental music.

Psalm 42.1-7 (a song of trust in God) and Isaiah 12.2-6 (a song of deliverance) are among the texts that can be sung in procession to the font. Settings include 'As the deer longs' by Bob Hurd and 'In the Lord I'll be ever thankful' by Jacques Berthier (with verses for cantor).

The Liturgy of Confirmation

The rubrics in the confirmation services suggest that 'a hymn, chant or litany' may be used before the bishop's prayer over the candidates. This might be sung on returning from the font, and could be an invocation of the Holy Spirit or a hymn or song of response to God or commitment to Christ.

The Sending Out

The final hymn or song must reinforce the dismissal liturgy, sending out the newly baptized and the congregation to 'shine as lights in the world to the glory of God the Father'. A hymn or song with a 'light' theme is an obvious choice, as is something about responding to God's call, or serving God in the world.

The hymns and songs in these tables have been chosen for a variety of reasons. Some, for example, have more implicit references to initiation, while others focus on the Christian journey, or God's sustaining love. Some of the items listed as suitable for baptisms are also worth considering for confirmation services, and vice versa. The number against the title is a suggestion about where each item might best be used, with the key given below. Many of these hymns and songs can be found in most major hymn books. Where a piece might be harder to track down we have identified at least one source, using the abbreviations given.

B Baptism (general)
C Confirmation (general)
1 Preparation
2 Liturgy of the Word
3 Procession to the font
4 Liturgy of baptism
5 Liturgy of confirmation
6 Intercessions
7 The Sending Out
8 When lots of children are present

Suggested hymns and songs

C 5,7	All for Jesus, all for Jesus
C 5	All I once held dear *CAHON, CMP, SG, SOF2, TS1*
B C 1,7	All my days (Beautiful Saviour) *CH4, CMP, SOF3, TS3*
C 1,7	All my hope on God is founded
C 5	All that I am, all that I do *CAHON, CFE, CH4, L*
C 5	All that I am I lay before you *CMP, SG, SOF2*
B 3	As the deer longs *CFE, CG, CH4, L*
B 4	At the dawning of creation *CAHON*
B C 3,7	At the name of Jesus
B C 4	Awake, awake, fling off the night
B 4	Baptized in water *CFE, CH4, HTC, L, SG*
B 4	Baptized into your name most holy *CH5*
C 5	Beautiful Lord, wonderful Saviour *CMP, SOF3, TS2*
C 1,7	Be thou my vision
B C 4,5	Born of the water, born of the Spirit *HTC*
B 4	Child of blessing, child of promise *CH4*
C 7	Christ be beside me *CFE, CH4, CH5, L*
C 1	Christ is the one who calls *CMP*
B 2,4	Christ, when for us you were baptized *AMNS, CP*
C 1,2,7	Christ who called disciples to him *SG*
C 1,7	Come down, O love divine
C 1,6	Come, Holy Spirit, descend on us (Bell) *CH4, CMP, L, TS3*
B 4	Conceiver of both heaven and earth *LFB*
C 5,7	Christians, lift up your hearts (The house of the Lord) *AMNS, LHON*
C 1,7,8	Colours of day *CMP, SOF*
B C 2,4,5	Do not be afraid, for I have redeemed you *CFE, CH4, CMP, L, CAHON, SOF3*
B 2,4	Empty, broken, here I stand (Kyrie eleison) *TS2*

B 4	Eternal God, we consecrate these children *AMNS, CP*	
B 4	Father, now behold us *CH5, HTC*	
C 2,7	Fight the good fight with all thy might	
C 2	Firmly I believe and truly	
B C 1,4,8	Give me joy in my heart (Sing hosanna)	
B 4	God the Father, name we treasure *AMNS, CP, HTC*	
C 7	Go forth for God *CH5, CP, NEH*	
C 6,7	Great is the darkness *CMP, SG, SOF, TS*	
C 2,5	Here is the place *CH4*	
B 8	He's got the whole world in his hands	
C 5	Holy Spirit, come, confirm us	
B C 4,5	I am a new creation *CAHON, CFE, CMP, SOF1, TS1*	
C 2,7	I'm not ashamed to own my Lord	
C 5	I bind unto myself today	
C 1,2,7	In Christ alone my hope is found *CMP, SOF3, TS3*	
B 3	In the Lord I'll be ever thankful *TZ*	
B 4	In token that thou shalt not fear *AMR*	
C 7,8	I, the Lord of sea and sky *CG, SOF2*	
C 2,5	It is the cry of my heart *CMP, SOF2*	
C 5	I will offer up my life *CH4, CMP, SG, SOF2, TS1*	
B C 1,3	Jesus is the name we honour *CMP, SOF, SG*	
B C 3	Just as I am, without one plea	
C 5,7	Light of the minds that know him *CH5, CMP, CP,*	
C 5	*HTC, SG*	
C 6	Longing for light (Christ, be our light) *CG*	
C 6,7	Lord, for the years	
C 5	Lord, I come to you (The power of your love) *CMP,*	
	SG, SOF2, TS1	
C 5,7	Lord of creation/Lord of all power	
B C 1,3,7,8	Lord, the light of your love (Shine, Jesus, Shine)	
C 5	Lord, we have come at your own invitation *CH4*	
7	Love songs from heaven *CMP, SOF2, TS2*	
C 2,5,7	May the mind of Christ, my Saviour	
C 6,7,8	Make me a channel of your peace	
C 5	My God, accept my heart this day	
B 4,7	Now is eternal life *AMNS, CH5, CP, NEH*	
B 4	Now through the grace of God we claim *CG, CH4, HTC*	
C 1	O breath of life, come sweeping through us *CMP, SOF*	
C 1,2	O God, you search me *CH4, L, SG, TS3*	
C 5,7	O Jesus, I have promised	
C 2,5	O Lord, you are the centre of my life *CFE, L, SG*	
C 1,5	O thou who camest from above	
B C 1,2,3,7,8	One more step along the world I go *CP*	
C 17	Over all the earth (Lord, reign in me) *CMP, SOF3, TS2*	
B 7	Out of darkness God has called us *CFE, L*	
C 5	Reign in me, sovereign Lord *CMP, SOF1, TS1*	

AMNS: Hymns Ancient & Modern New Standard (1983)

AMR: Hymns Ancient & Modern Revised (1950)

CAHON: Complete Anglican Hymns Old & New (2000)

CFE: Celebration Hymnal for Everyone (1994)

CG: Common Ground (1998)

CH4: Church Hymnary, 4th Edition (2005)

CH5: Church Hymnal, 5th Edition (2000)

CMP: Complete Mission Praise (2005 edition)

CP: Common Praise (2000)

HTC: Hymns for Today's Church (1987)

L: Laudate (1999)

NEH: New English Hymnal (1986)

SG: Sing Glory (1999)

SOF: Songs of Fellowship (Vols 1,2,3; 1991, 1998, 2003)

TS: The Source (Vols 1, 2, 3; 1998, 2001, 2005)

LFB: Love from Below (Vol. 3 of Wild Goose Songs) Iona Community 1992

TZ: Taizé: Songs for Prayer (1998)

B 3,4	River, wash over me *CMP, SOF1, TS1*	
C 1,5	Silent, surrendered, calm and still *CAHON*	
C 5,6	Spirit of the living God, fall afresh on me *CMP, SOF*	
B 1,4	Springs of water, bless the Lord *L*	
B C 4,5,7	Take my life, and let it be	
C 5,6	Take, O take me as I am *CH4, SG*	
B C 4,5	Take this moment, time and space *CFE, CG, CH4, CH5, L*	
B 2,8	There are hundreds of sparrows	
C 1,7	There's a spirit in the air *CP, SG*	
B 2,4	This is the truth which we proclaim *HTC, SG*	
B 4	Up from the waters *L*	
B 3	Water of life *CFE, L*	
B C 3,7	We are marching in the light of God	
B 2,4	We bring our children, Lord, today *CP*	
C 2,7	We have a gospel to proclaim	
B 4	We know that Christ is raised *CH4, HTC*	
B C 4,5	We turn to Christ alone *CMP*	
C 5	We turn to Christ anew *CH5*	
C 1,2,5	When I was lost (There is a new song) *CMP, SOF3, TS3*	
C 2,5,7	Will you come and follow me	
C 1	Ye that know the Lord is gracious *AMNS, CH4, CH5, CP, NEH*	
B 4	You have put on Christ *CFE, L*	

Using one hymn as a thread through the service

Sometimes it is possible (and it may be desirable) to use one song or hymn as a common thread throughout the service, using different verses at different places. This can be particularly helpful if lots of those in the congregation are new to church and unfamiliar with any songs or hymns: once they've learnt the song at one point in the service, they'll know it when it recurs later in the service. It can also break the singing up: little and often is sometimes more effective than one six-verse hymn (or worse – three six-verse hymns!)

For example, the modern hymn/song 'Great is the darkness' has three verses, which can be used as a thread through a Confirmation service. It wouldn't be the only song or hymn used in the service, but it can act as a common factor, helping to hold the service together.

After each verse, the refrain, 'Come, Lord Jesus . . . pour out your Spirit we pray.' prepares us for the next part of the service.

- Verse 1 ('Great is the darkness that covers the earth, oppression, injustice and pain . . .') can be sung as the bishop and candidates gather at the font following the Decision (and, if there are candidates for baptism, the signing with the cross)
- Verse 3 ('Great celebrations on that final day . . . then face to face we shall meet') can then sung after the prayer 'Almighty God, we thank you for our fellowship in the household of faith... make us ready for that day when the whole creation shall be made perfect . . .'
- Verse 2 ('May now your church rise with power and love . . . Help us bring light to this world . . .') can be sung at the end of the service, just before the giving of the lighted candles.

Other songs and hymns could be used in the same way.

There is no doubt that music presents its greatest challenge at 'stand-alone' services where, typically, congregations are likely to be less comfortable with singing than when baptism is administered within a church's regular worshipping framework. A practical approach which can work well in these situations is to have the music led by a small band of instrumentalists together with a lead singer. The right person cast in this role can give the congregation great confidence, especially if this is helped by choosing music with memorable refrains, or by the singer taking the first verse before inviting the congregation to join in thereafter.

The opportunities for the creative use of music within initiation liturgy are many, but as in all planning, care needs to be taken not to over-egg the pudding! Whatever music is chosen must enable the substance and drama of the liturgy to speak and not obscure it.

D9 Decision flowchart

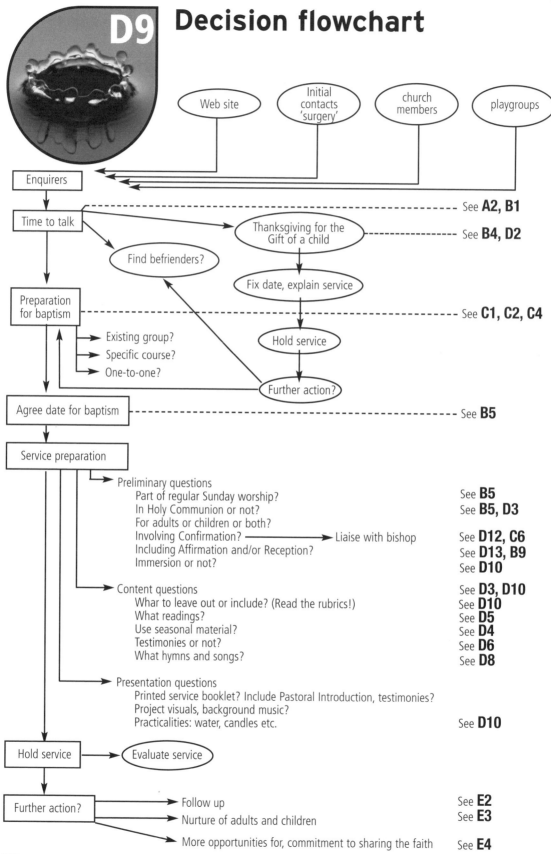

Web site

Initial contacts 'surgery'

church members

playgroups

Enquirers

Time to talk - See **A2, B1**

Thanksgiving for the Gift of a child - - - - - - - - - - See **B4, D2**

Find befrienders?

Fix date, explain service

Preparation for baptism - See **C1, C2, C4**

→ Existing group?
→ Specific course?
→ One-to-one?

Hold service

Further action?

Agree date for baptism - See **B5**

Service preparation

→ Preliminary questions
   Part of regular Sunday worship?   See **B5**
   In Holy Communion or not?   See **B5, D3**
   For adults or children or both?
   Involving Confirmation? ——————→ Liaise with bishop   See **D12, C6**
   Including Affirmation and/or Reception?   See **D13, B9**
   Immersion or not?   See **D10**

→ Content questions   See **D3, D10**
   Whar to leave out or include? (Read the rubrics!)   See **D10**
   What readings?   See **D5**
   Use seasonal material?   See **D4**
   Testimonies or not?   See **D6**
   What hymns and songs?   See **D8**

→ Presentation questions
   Printed service booklet? Include Pastoral Introduction, testimonies?
   Project visuals, background music?
   Practicalities: water, candles etc.   See **D10**

Hold service → Evaluate service

Further action?
→ Follow up   See **E2**
→ Nurture of adults and children   See **E3**
→ More opportunities for, commitment to sharing the faith   See **E4**

How to baptize

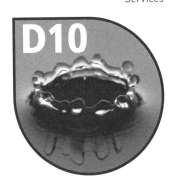

In essence baptism is quite simple. We baptize with water in the name of the Father, and of the Son and of the Holy Spirit. Any added words and symbolism serve to express the richness of the faith into which the candidate is baptized. At times the service required will be the very simplest form, as in an emergency baptism for someone who is very sick (see *CWCI*, page 102). At other times it is a great celebration of the gathered church. The practical considerations will vary according to the context. One of the joys of a baptism service is that it normally brings family and friends to church who are not regular worshippers. Making the service the best it can be is not just a matter of getting the practicalities right: it's about helping everyone to be focused on God rather than feeling lost or bewildered, or simply worried, by the service.

Use this chapter to find help with all the practical details, actions and movements involved in conducting a baptism. See Chapter D3 for the structure of the service into which these fit.

Getting ready

Advance preparation for the service ➤

As well as helping candidates or parents and godparents to understand the Baptism service, there will be a need for some form of practical preparation. That could be a full rehearsal, but it might be as simple as going through the service with some simple explanations of where you stand and what bits you say.

➤**C1 – C3**

Involving candidates or parents in the choosing of (some) hymns and songs is another way of helping them to engage with the service as an act of worship. In some situations (especially if the baptism is not taking place in a main Sunday service) it may be appropriate to involve the candidate or family in the choice of Bible reading too.

If the candidate is a toddler or older child it will be useful for the minister to get to know the child as much as possible. A chance to look at the font, an explanation of what will happen, and involving the child in discussions about who will hold them, or where (and on what) they will stand, will all help the child to feel confident.

Where to sit the family

Those unfamiliar with a church service may feel uncomfortable sitting right at the front of church. They have no one in front of them to give them clues about what to do, and may feel the whole church is watching them. If it is a baptism separate from the main Sunday act of worship this may not be so much of a problem, but at main services it may be better to reserve seats for them one or two rows further back.

Planning the movement of the service

Whatever type of font or pool is being used for the baptism, ➤ think about where to place the candidate or the parents and godparents so that they can see, but do not block everyone else's view.

➤**B10**

Encourage the congregation to stand and turn to face the font - if there's room, invite them to gather round. This might be the moment to encourage children in particular to make sure they can see.

D7 → Planning the flow of the service may include introducing physical movement, symbolizing the idea of journey. → There are two obvious points for purposeful movement:

- moving to and from the font – perhaps accompanied by a suitable song or hymn;
- a procession at the end of the service – possibly led by the candidate(s) carrying their lighted candles.

B10 → Practical preparations: a checklist →

- Water in a jug or ewer ready to pour dramatically into the font before the Prayer over the Water.
- Is the water warm enough? (Don't forget that stone fonts cool water very quickly.)
- Spare service sheets, as parents and godparents often leave them in their seats when they come forward.
- A card with the candidate's full name written clearly on it can act as an *aide-mémoire* at the crucial moment.
- Towel, purificator or tissue to dry the candidate after the baptism.
- Spare tissues if oil is being used.
- Minister's service sheet, preferably on laminated card or with plastic sleeves, to prevent damage from water or oil.
- Easter candle (or other large candle) in its place wherever the Decision is to take place.
- Matches or taper for lighting the Easter candle.
- Baptism candles for the candidates, ready to give them at the end of the service.

Certificates and register

The baptism certificate and cards for godpa
gister should be filled in immediately after the baptism – not before, in case there is an unexpected postponement.

D3 → The service itself →

Presentation of the candidates

The Presentation is printed just before the Decision, but the notes make clear that it may take place earlier, following the Introduction. The candidate(s) can be presented by godparents or sponsors, by those who have prepared them for baptism, or by a parish baptism visitor who is linked with that person or family. The *Common Worship* service does not spell out what presentation entails: it may be handled informally or more formally. Some churches take the opportunity to parade an infant candidate up and down the aisle so that everyone gets to see them. For older candidates, this might be the opportunity for testimony to be given. ← Those able to answer for themselves are asked if they wish to be baptized. The congregational commitment to welcoming and supporting the candidates underlines the fact that this is not just an individual act but the candidate is becoming part of the whole Body of Christ. ← At the baptism of children there are responses through which the parents and godparents are encouraged to draw them into the community of faith and help them in their journey.

←**D6**

←**C6**

The Decision

At the Decision a large candle may be lit, a visual connection with the spoken words of introduction. For churches that have an Easter candle, this is an appropriate point at which to light it.

This section of the service originates in the early practice of baptism candidates receiving exorcism. Now it is put more positively as a personal commitment to turn *from* all that pulls us away from God and to turn *towards* Christ. It is literally a turning point in the person's life, which is the basis for the new start expressed in baptism. The questions to candidates reflect this: three relate to what is turned *from*; three reflect what is turned *towards*. In some churches it may be possible to symbolize that 'turn' more dramatically with a literal turn around after the third question: perhaps a turn to face the Easter candle, or a turn from facing the west end of church towards the east end.

> **'In baptism God calls us out of darkness into his marvellous light.'**
>
> Holy Baptism (introduction to the Decision), *CWCI*, page 67

Signing of the cross and optional anointing with oil (first position)←

←**D7**

The cross is marked on the forehead, usually using the thumb. The minister makes the sign first (and says the words 'Christ claims you for his own, receive the sign of his cross'). Parents, godparents, and representatives of the congregation may then be invited to sign the candidate (the words are not repeated).

Where oil is used to make the sign of the cross, it is the Oil of Baptism.

The oil may be that which has been blessed at the Maundy Thursday service by the bishop. This gives a sense of unity with the wider church and connection with the bishop. The oil is normally put into a *stock*, a small container (often silver) with cotton wool or wadding soaked in oil. All those giving the sign of the cross can dip their thumb into it before making the sign. A supply of tissues is

> **'Where it has been agreed that oil will be used, pure olive oil, reflecting the practice of athletes preparing for a contest, may be used for the Signing with the Cross'**
>
> Note 10, *CWCI*, page 100

advisable for wiping hands afterwards. The signing with the cross may, optionally, take place in another position, immediately after the baptism itself. In this case the purpose and symbolism is different and so are the words.

[See *CWCI*, page 89]

The Prayer over the Water and Profession of Faith

The water

The water is either already in the font or is poured in just before the Prayer over the Water. Family, godparents, or church members can be involved if the water is brought in procession or poured in by someone other than the minister – or children can help to lift the ewer and pour it in.

The words

The Prayer over the Water expresses much of the theology and symbolism of baptism. The alternative seasonal and responsive forms add to this.

The profession of faith immediately preceding the baptism is normally the Apostles' Creed in question and answer form, but an alternative is provided.

The Baptism

Dipping or pouring?

The notes in *Christian Initiation* say

> 'A threefold administration of water (whether by dipping or pouring) is a very ancient practice of the Church and is commended as testifying to the faith of the Trinity in which candidates are baptized. Nevertheless, a single administration is also lawful and valid. The use of a substantial amount of water is desirable; water must at least flow on the skin of the candidate. The president may delegate the act of baptism to another lawful minister.'
>
> Note 12, page 100

The symbolism of dipping is bold – going down into the water as Christ died and was buried, and coming up from it raised with Christ as he rose from the dead. It has profound significance. Yet through the centuries it became marginalized in the Church of England, with normal practice being the pouring on of water. Despite this, the rubric in *The Book of Common Prayer* was always that dipping should be the norm albeit 'discreetly and warily', with an exception provided:

> 'But if they certify that the Child is weak, it shall suffice to pour Water upon it, saying the foresaid words.'
>
> *The Book of Common Prayer*, page 329

In recent years there has been an increase in appreciation of the symbolism of immersion or submersion and it is now more commonly offered as an option. Some new or reordered churches have a built-in baptistery, but for others temporary provision is necessary. ☛ **B10, D7**

Whether dipping or pouring is used, the water and its symbolism must remain central. ☛ **D7** Any other symbols may enhance our understanding and enrich our worship, but must not overpower this central act. It is the water and accompanying words that effect baptism, not the signing of the cross or the use of oil. Therefore their use, although helpful, needs to be recognized as supplementary. The way the baptism is administered needs to reflect this.

Infant baptism with pouring

Each minister will develop their own method of holding the child so that the infant is secure and one hand is free for administering the water. The water is poured over the head liberally with the hand, or a shell (a Christian symbol linked to baptism, which pilgrims used to wear as a form of identification).

Adult baptism with pouring

An adult or older child will stand by the font (on a stool or similar, if necessary) with head bowed over the edge to facilitate the pouring of water, which may be done with the hand or with a shell, or, for a more dramatic effect, a suitable jug. If you are intending to use a lot of water, then a towel round the shoulders of the candidate can be useful.

Infant baptism with immersion

Fonts in many old churches are big enough for immersing infants – earlier practice of immersion is probably the reason for their size. The baby can be cradled in the water and water poured over the head, or the child can be held securely and lowered into the water and raised. A good grasp and confident handling will help the child to feel secure. Warm water and a warm environment are preferable. It may be possible for the child to be baptized naked. In any case, towels and dry clothing need to be at hand. This provides a great opportunity for the child to re-appear clad in its christening gown.

Adult baptism with immersion

The type of pool being used will affect the practice. Clearly using a swimming pool, river or sea, or a purpose-made baptistery, will enable the candidate to walk right down into the water. The person baptizing them is either awaiting them or accompanies them. Depending on the depth of water the candidate can stand or kneel and have water poured over their head, or can be securely held and lowered and raised forwards, or lowered backwards with head and shoulders supported. In small pools the candidate can sit, stand or kneel, while plentiful amounts of water are poured over, or lowered and raised if there is enough room.

The candidate will need to wear appropriate clothing that ensures modesty, and a bathing costume can be worn underneath. Towels, sheets or bathrobes need to be available for when they come out of the water and a suitable place provided for them to change. If warm enough they can remain at the poolside until other candidates have been baptized and until a hymn can be sung while they go to get changed. The minister will also have to change, if he or she has been standing in the water to do the baptism, so it may help to have an assistant minister present to continue the service while this is done.

Health and safety issues such as precautions against slipping on wet floors, keeping the environment warm enough to prevent chills, and assistance when necessary to help in the lowering and raising of a candidate to protect the minister from back or other injury should be borne in mind. Microphones and other electrical equipment in the vicinity of water are a particular hazard to bear in mind.

Any problems with improvised pools will not necessarily be foreseen without a test run, which is recommended. Water is heavy, and the sides of pools have been known to give way. The way the pool is filled, the method of heating the water and how long it takes to prepare, and the way the pool is emptied all need to be planned carefully and preferably tried out before the baptism. It is also important to work out how the minister and candidate will make a dignified entrance and exit, and how the baptism will be performed.

Signing of the cross and optional anointing with oil (second position)►

►D7

If the sign of the cross is made after the baptism, rather than at the Decision, the Oil of Chrism may be used. This fragrant perfumed oil is a symbol of the Spirit empowering and equipping for the life ahead, which is the theme of the prayer which immediately follows baptism. In order to enhance this symbol some churches like to use the oil lavishly, either pouring it on so that the fragrance is released and the sense of blessing is seen to be a generous outpouring, or at least making a larger 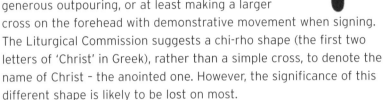 cross on the forehead with demonstrative movement when signing. The Liturgical Commission suggests a chi-rho shape (the first two letters of 'Christ' in Greek), rather than a simple cross, to denote the name of Christ – the anointed one. However, the significance of this different shape is likely to be lost on most.

Clothing►

►D7

Although it has become traditional to wear white for baptism, there is more significance in changing clothes *after* the baptism itself. If baptism is by immersion then this becomes a practical necessity, but it is also a visual symbol of the fact that the candidate has now put on Christ (Romans 13.14) and is being clothed with the armour of God (Ephesians 6.11) and the characteristics of those who are God's chosen ones (Colossians 3.12,14).

If this practice is followed then the candidate is baptized in everyday clothing or a simple robe made for the purpose, and then changes into white as soon after the baptism as practicable. However many places regard clothing in white as unnecessary (or even discourage it) where it puts a financial strain on the candidates or their families – especially for adults who are unlikely to wear such clothes normally.

'Where there are adult baptisms by immersion, the Baptist tradition of a white toweling dressing gown offered to the newly baptized candidates may well stand for the ancient tradition of clothing in modern form.'

Commentary, *CWCI*, page 337

The Commission and Prayers

Those present are reminded that the newly baptized need help and encouragement, and one or more prayers are said. Those old enough to answer for themselves are assured of God's promises to them and encouraged in their journey. For older candidates the commission can include a set of personal commitments given in question and answer form. The whole commissioning section is normally done with the congregation standing.

Intercessory prayers may come at this point or after the Welcome and Peace. They may sometimes be led by godparents, sponsors, a family member or a baptism visitor.

The Welcome and Peace

There is one Lord, one faith, one baptism:
N and N, by one Spirit we are all baptized into one body.
We welcome you into the fellowship of faith;
We are children of the same heavenly father;
We welcome you.

The welcome is an important part of the service as it expresses the new belonging of the candidate to Christ's Body, his Church.

When baptism takes place in a main service the gathered Body of Christ is present and the welcome is immediate and embraces the newly baptized. This is ideally a sincere and warm welcome with applause and enthusiastic saying of the congregational acclamation. In some churches the newly baptized is led (or carried if it is an infant) into the midst of the congregation as applause is given.

B5➤ When the baptism is not part of the main service, or takes place in another parish, in deanery or diocesan services or in the cathedral, the welcome into the local congregation may be done by using Celebration after an Initiation Service outside the Parish (pages 182-3). ➤ This is relatively brief and can be added to any service at the next convenient opportunity.

The Peace can be shared whether or not the Welcome takes place, as an expression of our belonging and oneness in Christ.

D7➤ ## The giving of a candle➤

The type and size of candle vary but it is good to give something significant that can be relit for baptismal anniversaries or birthdays. It is lit from the Easter candle or other large candle that was lit at the Decision. It can be given by the minister or by a representative of the congregation or a baptism visitor. If the baptism party have returned to their seats after the baptism then a godparent or another family member can go to receive the candle where it is lit and bring it to the candidate, or the whole baptism party can return to the font or the place where the Decision was made and lead the congregation out as the final act of the service. This gives meaning to the sending out to 'walk in this light all the days of your life' and 'shine as a light to the world to the glory of God the Father'.

[CWCI, pages 102-5] # Emergency Baptism

A lay person may be the minister of baptism in an emergency, usually when it is thought that death might be imminent. Afterwards they should inform those responsible for the pastoral care of that person. The form is very brief consisting of the pouring on of water with the baptismal formula, with options for adding preparatory sentences of scripture, signing of the cross, a brief prayer over the water, the Lord's Prayer and other prayers and a blessing. However it is essentially only the pouring of water and baptismal formula that are required. The Notes (page 105) describe the service to be held in church if the person lives.

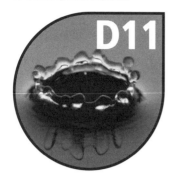

D11

Admission of the baptized to Communion

Rites on the Way included this service for those parishes that have the bishop's permission to admit persons to Holy Communion before confirmation. This material forms a helpful resource for such parishes and will need to be read carefully and adapted to local circumstances. The status of this material is 'commended' which means that other texts may still be used - some parishes or dioceses may have texts which have been refined over time, and which they do not wish to abandon.

A6, B2, B8 ➤

[*CWCI*, page 188]

The notes ➤

The notes encourage the congregation to be aware that people are being prepared for receiving communion. The policy will have been fully discussed when permission was first sought from the bishop to admit people to communion before confirmation. Congregations change over time, however, and the use of this material will provide a useful reminder of the church's policy. It is of course desirable that those being prepared are prayed for by name in the services of the church. The notes also suggest that a display with pictures be put up in the church. A card could be produced for members of the congregation to pray for these people. If this type of approach is taken, it will also be necessary to do the same for confirmation candidates.

There is concern in the notes to make clear this is not a baptism or confirmation. Thus it prohibits the use of water, oil, the laying on of hands, or the presence of a bishop! The texts themselves include enough to make clear the action of the church. Though the service is the equivalent of first Communion, it is not necessary to acquire all the secondary symbolism that goes with that in some parts of the church, but it might be good to encourage wearing something white in remembrance of baptism. Clearly this will be the main Sunday service and one that some will anticipate greatly.

The texts

Pastoral introduction

This is a helpful introduction to what is going on. The directions imply that the congregation has the text before them and has read it in their service sheet. This is only one option, and could also be used as a spoken introduction to the service.

The welcome and the questions

The welcome can be used at the beginning of the service, or before the Peace. The questions (on page 192) are an alternative to be used before the Peace. The welcome proclaims the nature of the Church and our mode of celebration. It introduces and welcomes those who are here to receive communion for the first time. The decision about which text to use will depend on the style and custom of the church and possibly the particular candidates in question. It is worth noting that the question to the congregation is a call for prayer and support, and the question to the candidates, rather than asking about faith or discipleship, assumes both and merely asks whether they wish to receive Holy Communion.

Eucharistic provision

The service provides:

- a petition to add to the prayers of intercession;
- a particular form for the Peace;
- prayers for the preparation of the table;
- a proper preface;
- a post communion prayer;
- directions for the dismissal.

Some of this material is specially written for the purpose (for instance, the petition at the intercessions) and some is existing material suggested for this context (such as the words at the Peace).

Pastoral introduction

'Today we welcome to Communion *N and N* who share faithfully and regularly in our worship. A person is admitted to communion on the basis of their baptism, the sign and pledge of incorporation into the death and resurrection of Christ and the new life of the kingdom of God. *N and N* have been baptized, and today they receive the sacrament of the body and blood of Christ with us. They are taking a new step in the life to which God has called them in baptism and which we trust they will later affirm in confirmation. We welcome them and look forward to learning with and from them as we journey together on the Way of Christ.'

CWCI, page 189

The Welcome

We are God's pilgrim people.
We share in the story of God's love for the world,
God's love in Christ, calling us to himself,
God's love in the Spirit, giving strength for our
  journey of faith.
We celebrate this love in word and song,
we feed on Jesus in bread and wine
and make him known through our life together.

As the people of God in this place, we share the responsibility of encouraging one another in our worship and supporting one another in our discipleship, by our example and our prayers.

N and N, we welcome you in Jesus' name to receive communion with us.

At the Dismissal

Those admitted to communion may be invited forward, and the following may be said.
God has touched us with his love
and nourished us at his table.
As God's pilgrim people,
may we continue to explore the Way of Christ,
and grow in friendship with God,
in love for his people, and in serving others.

Those who have been admitted to communion may lead the following

To a troubled world
peace from Christ.

To a searching world
love from Christ.

To a waiting world
hope from Christ.

At the preparation of the table it is suggested that those welcomed lead the prayers for preparation. Likewise at the dismissal the suggestion is that those admitted lead the dismissal.

This will all have to be tailored to suit the particular group involved, and of course, it is desirable to involve the children themselves in the planning of the whole service.

What the service doesn't mention ...

Certificates

The regulations for the admission of the baptized to Holy Communion make clear that each person so welcomed should be given some certificate or other proof of their admission (such as a note on their baptism certificate). It may be appropriate to present the children with these certificates as part of the liturgical welcome, and this might be done after the welcome or questions (whichever is used). Whoever gives the certificates, and however it is handled, it will be important to avoid the impression that this is some sort of 'graduation' or that the children have achieved a certain level of understanding, which now qualifies them to receive communion. It must be clear that the certificate is proof that they have been admitted, *not* proof that they have successfully completed a preparation course. It may help to talk about 'cards' rather than 'certificates'.

Applause

It will also be natural for the congregation to greet the newly admitted with applause. Again, this will need to be handled in such a way that it is plain that this is the applause of welcome (similar to that offered at a baptism) rather than applause earned by achievement.

Parents

The decision about whether a child will be admitted to communion will normally be taken by the incumbent, in consultation with each child's parents. If the children are to be formally presented to the congregation before their welcome, the parents (or godparents or sponsors) may be the obvious people to do that.

Confirmation in practice

D12

Before the service

Bishops, incumbents and others planning confirmation services need to have quite a lot of information to help them to prepare. Bishops often send out a letter asking for information like this. The headings in this section could be used as a checklist.

Who will be there?

The most important people are the candidates. Who are they? Adults? Teenagers? If so – what ages? From a long-term church background, or not? Anyone preaching at a confirmation, choosing hymns or leading the intercessions will need to bear in mind the fact that candidates will be coming with a great range of motives for being confirmed. ➤ Getting the candidates to give some testimony to their spiritual journey will help to show the range of reasons why people get confirmed, and this can include a mixture of spoken and written testimony. ➤

➤**A2, A6**

➤**D6**

Will there be baptisms?

Are there adults – or infants – to be baptized? Should this be done at the confirmation service?

Advantages:

- Shows the bishop is engaged in true sacramental initiation.
- Reinforces the meaning of renewing baptismal vows for everyone else.
- Adds fairly powerful drama to the occasion.
- If there are both adults and infants (sometimes in the families of those being confirmed), the service demonstrates the core meaning of baptism which is common to adult, infant and child candidates.

Disadvantages:

- Candidates may want to be baptized in their 'home' church or with a larger number of friends present than may be possible for instance at a deanery confirmation.
- Some may think it makes the service longer and more complex

CW Christian Initiation provides one basic service, Baptism and Confirmation within a Celebration of Holy Communion (pages 107–23), with instructions on what changes to make if there are no candidates for baptism (Confirmation within a Celebration of Holy Communion, pages 124–5) and if there is no Holy Communion (pages 126–7). The presumption is that there will be both baptisms and Holy Communion.

Will the service include Holy Communion?

A key practical issue which people organizing a confirmation service need to think about is whether it will be a Communion service or not. There are things to be said for and against this.

For:

A6

- Holy Communion is the central act of the Church's worship, the natural setting for the range of things which people think may happen in confirmation.
- The expectation in the structure of the service is that it will be in the context of Holy Communion.
- The basic core of the service will be familiar, at least to church members.
- For those who do not yet receive communion, it links confirmation to first communion, and for some reinforces the idea of restoring what they see as an ancient practice when baptism included the laying on of hands, anointing, and first communion.

Against:

- Many candidates want to make their first communion in their home parish.
- It makes the service longer (but does this matter?).
- For the increasing number of candidates who already receive communion, confirmation is not the gateway to first communion.
- Family members and friends who do not receive communion may feel excluded.

How complicated can the service be?

[See *CWCI*, page 107]

The clear structure of the service means that it is not difficult to include

- The baptism of both infants and adults
- Affirmation of Baptismal Faith
- Reception into the Communion of the Church of England.

Even though none of these require the presence of the bishop, it is good to see the bishop involved in a range of things like this which fall within the Church's policy on initiation. Affirmation and Reception fit in well after the confirmation, before the prayer for all those on whom hands have been laid. There is also a fully worked-out order of service for Baptism and Confirmation within a Vigil Service on the Eve of Pentecost, beginning with the Service of

D4 Light.

Consultation

The draft of the service might come from the bishop's office or from the incumbent, using *Visual Liturgy* for instance. Ideas for songs and other content may come from the candidates themselves. Wherever it comes from there will be things to decide, perhaps by exchanging annotated copies of the draft. The bishop has the last word – it's his service – and needs to control the timetable. The final text should have no options, no rubrics saying *'the bishop may...'* Issues will include:

- The **ordering of the service** and where baptism and confirmation are to be administered.
- **Seating:** Some bishops prefer candidates to be seated in one or more front rows, with lay sponsors beside or just behind them. Sometimes other members of the family will be with them. Others prefer candidates to sit with their families wherever they wish, and sometimes invite families and friends to stand at the moment of confirmation. Another option is for candidates and families to be in a series of rows working back from the front, with candidates in end seats, so that they can come out easily.
- **Dress:** Bishops can wear alb and stole, with or without cope or chasuble or mitre, or Convocation robes. White is the best colour, as this is at root a baptismal occasion.
- **Choreography**: Since the bishop confirms standing (the assumption in the service text, as it is a prayer), walking along a row of kneeling candidates, a chair in the centre should not be necessary. When empty it gets in the way. The bishop may need somewhere to sit for the readings and possibly testimony, but that could be at the side.
- **Collect and readings:** The collect may be one of the Sunday ones or may be a baptismal or seasonal one. ➤ The readings should be of the Sunday (midweek services may be of the previous Sunday, or sometimes a saint's day).
- **Music**: Are there items to suit the different congregations represented?➤
- **Presentations**: Ideally these are done by lay sponsors, with smaller numbers of candidates being presented individually by name, each standing (or coming out to the front) as their names are called. If there are no sponsors, or if numbers are large, then they may be presented in groups with words like 'Bishop, from the parish of St. John's I present five candidates for confirmation, one of whom, Susan, is to be baptized.'
- **Testimonies**: The bishop may prefer these at the Presentation if he wants to refer to them in his sermon.➤

'The places where baptism and confirmation are administered should be determined after consultation between the bishop and the parish priest. Nevertheless, wherever possible all candidates should make the profession of baptismal faith (even when there are no candidates for baptism) at the place of baptism, the font.'

Note 1, *CWCI*, page 128

➤**D5**

➤**D8**

➤**D6**

One bishop writes: 'We need to end up with me facing the congregation across the font, with any baptismal candidates on my left side, with other confirmation and renewal candidates circling the font as close to as possible, with sponsors in a ring immediately behind their candidates, and (asl will coach them) with the rest of the congregation **D10** packing in behind them. Little kiddies may sit on the floor almost under the font. Some of this arrangement may affect how you visualize marching to the font – for instance, I would for preference go last; but if I have then to fight my way through seventeen candidates to get to the font, I would rather go first. Similarly, in some places the choir may lead off, but in others they will simply be in the way when they get there.'

'The Paschal candle, or another large candle, may be lit at the Decision and individual candles may be lit from it and given to candidates, including the newly confirmed, as part of the Sending Out. The giving of lighted candles to the newly baptized may take place at an earlier stage in the rite after the administration of baptism, in which case candles are not given to the newly confirmed.'

Note 14, *CWCI*, page 131

- **The Decision** and the **Profession of Faith**: The assumption is that the form in the service will usually be used.
- **The Procession to the Font**, managing the choreography following at the end of this in such a way that people can see what is happening.
- **If there is a baptism**, the way in which the Signing with the Cross is to be done. Is it to be done at the front? Do sponsors (and family?) join in?
- Again if there is a baptism, details of the mode of baptism, provision of towels, drying and changing arrangements if needed.
- How is the **signing or sprinkling** of non-baptismal candidates to be handled?

'The candidates for confirmation who have previously been baptized (together with those affirming their baptismal faith or seeking reception) may come forward to the font and sign themselves with water, or the bishop may sprinkle them.'

Confirmation service rubric, *CWCI*, page 117

- The **practicalities** of the actual confirmation, where candidates kneel, whether sponsors stand behind them, perhaps holding a card with the candidate's name on, and what help the bishop needs with anointing, if that happens.
- If there is **communion**, the bishop may need reassurance that things like the laying up of vessels and taking care of consecrated remains are all dealt with.
- **Candles:** if these are given out, how and when is this to happen?

On the day

Before the service

The bishop may need to:

- sign books and certificates for the candidates (if that is not done afterwards while meeting them and their families);
- sign confirmation registers, baptism register and service register;
- receive a diocesan form from each parish with details of the candidates;
- run through the final order of service;
- discover how to pronounce unusual Christian names, any family relationships among the candidates, and any disabilities;

- brief a chaplain (if any);
- briefly greet the candidates to put them at their ease;
- have space for prayer.

During the service

- Most bishops expect to preside from when they enter, so it works best if notices happen before the entry procession, ending with the announcement of the first hymn.
- Be prepared for the bishop to do things in a different way from your usual practice – and perhaps to learn from it.
- Again, at the Welcome, many bishops invite the candidates to face the congregation and encourage applause.

After the service

- If the Bishop is signing books etc, is there a table at which he can sit to do so?
- Will it be possible to take individual or group photos at the font?
- Will certificates be given to candidates immediately, or saved for the following Sunday in their home churches?

This means the end is the best place, so all receive candles and none need concern themselves about when they are to be put out. If there are large numbers, it may be easier to give them during the hymn, rather than cause a hiatus.

One bishop invites comment, for instance, on this idea: 'Acclamation: there is no congregational response to the climactic moment of baptism. If you like the idea, I would take each newly baptized person by the hand, raise that hand up, and call to the congregation 'Praise God for Eleanor's baptism' – and they would shout in response 'Alleluia! Amen!' Or I would be open to other acclamations, if you want to suggest them.'

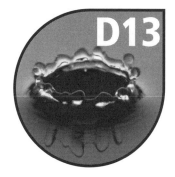

D13

Affirmation and Reception

Affirmation of Baptismal Faith and Reception into the Communion of the Church of England are new services in *Common Worship*, and likely to be less familiar to most worshippers than the services of baptism and confirmation.

In most situations, Reception into the Communion of the Church of England is likely to be a fairly rare element to incorporate into worship.

B9 →

Where to find Affirmation of Baptismal Faith and Reception into the Communion of the Church of England
Affirmation: *CWCI*, pages 197–210
Reception, pages 211–24
Like all the other *Common Worship* services, they are available on the Church of England web site and as part of the *Visual Liturgy* service planning software.

Affirmation of Baptismal Faith is intended for an individual who wishes to affirm a new step forward in fulfilling their baptism – it is not to be confused with the Corporate Renewal of Baptismal Vows (which is provided for separately on pages 193–6)

Affirmation of Baptismal Faith, on the other hand, is more likely to be a relatively frequently used service, providing as it does, an opportunity for those who have already been confirmed to recognize publicly a new step forward in faith. This might include those who were confirmed at a relatively young age, then drifted away from church during their teenage years, but now have come back to a more active faith later in life. It is also useful because it can take place more than once, allowing for individuals to mark several different stages of growth in faith, perhaps over several decades, but relating each stage back to the foundation of baptism into Christ.

Key decisions

The primary decision is whether the act of affirmation and/or reception is to be celebrated in the normal parish act of worship (whether a Eucharist or Service of the Word) or whether it is to be part of a service of confirmation.

Both affirmation and reception can be presided over by a bishop or a priest (unless a candidate for reception is a priest, in which case the diocesan bishop should preside), so there is plenty of scope for flexibility.

Affirmation or Reception as part of a confirmation service

Often affirmation or reception will most naturally be included in a confirmation service, where the bishop will be presiding. This makes a wonderful service, but working out how it all fits together need not be daunting.

Structure of the service

Parts of the service involving affirmation and reception candidates have references to the candidates in *italics*. An asterisk indicates the parts of the service that only happen if there are baptisms. Elements in square brackets are optional.

Presentation of the candidates

All candidates

The Decision

All candidates

Signing with the Cross*

Baptismal candidates only*

Prayer over the Water*

All candidates gather at the font

Profession of Faith

All candidates, with congregation

Baptism*

Baptismal candidates only*

Declarations (at the font)

Affirmation and *reception candidates*

[Signing with water from the font – or sprinkling]

[Confirmation, *affirmation* and *reception candidates*]

Confirmation – at 'the place of confirmation'

Confirmation candidates

Affirmation of Baptismal Faith

Affirmation candidates

Reception into the Communion of the Church of England

Reception candidates

[Commission]

[*All candidates;* this can alternatively be used before the Blessing and the Giving of a Lighted Candle]

[Intercessions]

[When there is no Eucharist these can follow the Welcome and Peace on page 120 of *CWCI*]

Welcome* and Peace

The newly baptized are welcomed* before the Peace

[Liturgy of the Eucharist]

[If the service includes Communion]

[Giving of a lighted candle]

[*All candidates*]

Though such a service can be a great celebration of God at work in people's lives in many different ways and at different stages, it can also get extremely long, which can be difficult, especially if there are many visitors present who are not used to church services. Great care is needed in putting the service together to make sure that the key elements are allowed to dominate and 'frills' are kept to a minimum.

Affirmation or Reception in a Sunday Service

Affirmation or Reception can take place in a normal service in the local church, presided over by the parish priest. In this case there might only be one candidate and the Affirmation or Reception will be part of a normal Eucharist or Service of the Word. Ideally, Affirmation or Reception would take place during a service that includes baptism, but this will not always be possible, or desirable, for pastoral or practical reasons.

If incorporating Affirmation or Reception into a normal Sunday service, the main things to remember are that the normal Prayers of Penitence and Creed (or Affirmation of Faith) are omitted.

CW Christian Initiation gives worked out orders of service for Holy Communion incorporating Affirmation (pages 197ff.) and Reception (pages 211f.). The notes at the end of each service gives guidelines for incorporating either into a Service of the Word or Morning or Evening Prayer.

Edward is 8 and is being baptized at St Edwin's, having started coming to church after a school visit to the church. His mum, Sheila, has also been coming to church. She was brought up Roman Catholic and was confirmed at 12, but hasn't really been to church since, until Edward showed an interest. She now feels her faith has been renewed and she wants to be part of St Edwin's. Paul, another member of St Edwin's congregation, has been a regular churchgoer all his life, but after a recent Emmaus course, is excited that his faith has 'come alive' in a new way and he wants to show it. He too has been confirmed.

At Edward's baptism, all three of them spoke briefly about what God was doing in their lives. Paul affirmed his baptismal faith, and Sheila was received into the Church of England.

What happens at Affirmation or Reception?

At **Affirmation** services, water may be used to remind people of their baptism, and afterwards the presiding priest or bishop extends his or her hands and prays over all candidates for affirmation and then lays a hand on the head of each candidate (as at confirmation) saying,

> *N*, may God renew his life within you that you may confess his name this day and for ever. Amen.

At **Reception**, the presiding priest or bishop extends his or her hands and prays over all candidates for reception and then 'takes the hand' of each person to be received – effectively giving them a welcoming handshake – and says,

> *N*, we recognize you as a member of the one, holy catholic and apostolic church; and we receive you into the communion of the Church of England in the name of the Father, and of the Son, and of the Holy Spirit. Amen.

If candidates use significant amounts of water with which to sign themselves (or even dip themselves), it is important to remember that however significant for the person, this is a personal reminder of the baptism that has already taken place, and that no words are used.

[*CWCI*, page 350]

Section

E

PILGRIMS
The end - or just the beginning?

These three stories may sound familiar ...

Tracey and Ian asked for their son, **Ben**, to be christened at the church where they had been married, in the village two miles from where they currently lived. They sounded enthusiastic about coming to family services, and came to church a couple of times before Ben's baptism, but never appeared again afterwards, although the church sent Ben cards on the anniversary of his baptism, and information about activities for children.

Mark and Holly had both been regular churchgoers when they were young, but since mid-teens had only attended their parish church for carol services. Their daughter, **Justine**, heard about baptism from the vicar at her church school when she was seven. She went home and asked her mum if she had been baptized, and when her mum explained that she hadn't, Justine decided she wanted to find out more. Holly phoned the vicar, and the phone call resulted in a few visits to talk to Justine and her parents about baptism. Justine was baptized and began to bring her parents to church. Soon she joined the choir, and Holly became more involved, first with helping with the children, and then on the church council.

Sue asked to be confirmed after she moved to a new parish. She had been a churchgoer for some years, but had missed out on being confirmed with her friends in her teens because of family moves. She attended the small confirmation classes, and was confirmed a few months before she got married. She continued to attend church for a while, but because of her husband's business and other family commitments, she came less and less frequently.

A destination or a step on a journey?

Because of their cultural heritage, there are many families for whom a christening is a major family event to celebrate the birth of their child, and her 'official' acceptance into the wider family and community. This involves the church, but after the service is over, it is only the immediate family who are involved in the child's upbringing. For an older child, who has not been baptized before, deciding to belong to the church may be a significant step and the sense of being baptized into the Christian family will be much clearer.

Many adults who ask for baptism will see it as part of their ongoing journey with God, and will want it to be another step on a road which will probably lead to confirmation and perhaps a commitment to serving God in a specific way.

Clearly there is a range of expectations about how Christian initiation connects with the rest of a person's life. The pastoral introduction to the Baptism service says

> 'Baptism marks the beginning of a journey with God which continues for the rest of our lives.'
>
> CWCI, page 62

There are two key perspectives to bear in mind:

- becoming more like Jesus – Christian initiation is about personal transformation;
- joining a community – Christian initiation is about building relationships.

How can we help those who come for baptism or confirmation, whatever age they are, to see it not as an ending, but as just the beginning?

Emphasizing a new beginning

Here are some ideas as a starting point:

Children

- The initial preparation, ☞ whether done as individuals or in a group, could involve other church members, ideally others who are bringing up children in the church family (or who remember doing so).☞

  ☞C1 – C3

  ☞C6
- In the preparation, discuss how Christian families live differently from others in the wider community.
- Send (or hand-deliver) cards on the anniversary of the baptism, perhaps delivered by someone who helped to prepare the families for the baptism.

C6→
- Send invitations to whatever activities are available for children in the parish, and to family services – personal invites where possible.→
- Hold an annual tea party or something similar for those who have been baptized during the year, with activities and games for the children and culminating in a family-friendly act of worship.
- Run a course on parenting and invite the parents of children who have been baptized recently.
- Make children's books of Bible stories and prayers and similar resources available to buy or borrow, perhaps using and advertising them in all-age services.

Older children, teens and adults

C1 – C3→
- The initial preparation → could involve people as leaders who have recently been baptized or confirmed, and who can share what the early stages of the journey have been like for them.
- In preparation, challenge candidates to think through how they might go against the flow of contemporary culture.
- Being part of a group is vital, whether it is a continuation of the preparation group, or a different one. Going through baptism or confirmation preparation together may be more of a uniting factor than age.
- Is an away-day or a retreat together before a confirmation possible?
- Make resources available – books, CDs, music or websites.
- Provide the encouragement and support of other Christians, whether in church or in small groups or a one-to-one

C3→
 relationship. → A sponsor for a teenager can be another teenager, or someone who has more of a 'grandparent' role. This would ideally include opportunities for praying together, as well as talking about things.
- Encourage the newly initiated to be involved in the church community by taking a responsible part, such as helping to plan a service, being a PCC member – not just taking the collection!
- Encourage involvement in mission. Could part of the preparation include reaching out to others in some way?

Food for the hungry

From time to time each congregation should review how well it is incorporating and feeding those who have been baptized and confirmed. A genuine welcome and concern, remembering who people are, and providing the spiritual food that they need, all make a big difference.

Questions for discussion

1. Do we know people like Tracey, Ian and Ben, Holly, Mark and Justine, and Sue? What can we learn from their stories?

2. How have we resisted the temptations to give up on the journey?

3. What criteria should a church council use in evaluating the church's 'success' in post-initiation care, integration and growth?

E2

Growing in the faith

Baptism or confirmation is not the end of Christian discipleship and learning, but just a step on a long journey.

In churches that are fortunate enough to have a number of children, there is usually some structured form of learning for children and teenagers, through activities and groups for different ages. The quality may vary (as so many things do in church life) but the structure is often there.

Where the numbers of children are small, and there are no groups, then a different approach is necessary. Perhaps there are groups or activities in neighbouring churches that a child or teenager could be connected with or encouraged to join? Or maybe a more personal 'one-to-one' approach will be necessary.

Paul wrote to the Romans:

'I appeal to you therefore, brothers and sisters, by the mercies of God, to present your bodies as a living sacrifice, holy and acceptable to God, which is your spiritual worship. Do not be conformed to this world, but be transformed by the renewing of your minds, so that you may discern what is the will of God – what is good and acceptable and perfect.'

Romans 12.1–2

For young children, the godparents are those particularly charged with the ongoing nurture of the candidate, and so the most realistic approach may be to find ways of supporting and helping godparents.

For newly initiated adults the structures and patterns for helping them to grow are not always so obvious, and even in churches where evangelism is a priority, nurture is often neglected.

Whatever age we are, being a disciple of Jesus touches every aspect of our lives – how we do our work, how we treat our friends and family, how we use our money, even how we think.

This chapter suggests some of the ways that a new Christian can be helped to grow, intellectually, spiritually and as a member of the wider Church.

Personal Bible study

The value of regular personal Bible study should have been taught in the preparation course, but without guilt-inducing legalism. A wide range of personal Bible study notes is available, some tailored for relatively new believers.

Study Bibles, commentaries and concordances will be helpful to some. And how many Christians realize that numerous versions of the Bible are accessible though the Internet, often with search facilities?

Try
www.biblegateway.com
bible.oremus.org

Personal relationships for discipleship

Sponsors can continue to play a role in the ongoing journey of the newly baptized, keeping in touch on a regular basis to share prayer requests, insights from the Bible, and various hints and tips about the Christian life.

The relationship between Paul and Timothy is often cited as a model for this, or the teaching and encouragement given to Apollo by Priscilla and Aquila.

[Acts 16.1-3, 2 Timothy 2.2, Acts 18.25-26]

> Julie realized that she and her sponsor Mary both worked in the same part of town. They agreed to meet up for lunch once a week, each one bringing a prayer request, and something learnt from the Bible in the past week. They eventually became firm friends.

Some churches may wish to set up a formal mentoring scheme. But a lighter touch may be more appropriate – for example, an encouragement from the leadership of the church for a sponsor and candidate to meet at least monthly for coffee and chat during the first year after the baptism.

Nurture groups

Many Christians benefit from a small group to help them grow in their Christian life. Bible study groups, 'house groups', cell groups – the name and particular focus may vary from church to church, but the basic idea is common, either as a regular part of church life or in particular seasons, such as Lent groups.

Some parishes might prefer to keep the newly baptized together in a group that will be focused, at least initially, on their specific needs; some of the Emmaus material is suitable for this. Other churches will seek to integrate these new members into existing groups.

There are plenty of off-the-peg courses to resource small groups. Care needs to be taken to oversee the direction of groups over a number of years and relate this to the needs and priorities of the congregation. Series that work through books of the Bible, chapter by chapter, might alternate with series based on a more thematic approach. Some churches link their midweek study to the topics taught on Sundays.

For some new Christians the workplace, rather than the church, will be the easier place to meet regularly with other Christians for Bible study, prayer and fellowship, so don't forget to encourage this with individuals for whom it might be appropriate.

The place of the sermon

For many Christians it is likely that the sermon will be the main teaching event with which they will be involved. Clergy and Readers will need to consider the overall teaching and preaching programme, making sure that the 'level' of sermons, the modes of communication, and the topics tackled are appropriate for newer Christians as well as those who are more established in the faith.

Printed and other media

The worldwide Church is an excitingly diverse community – many new Christians are encouraged and inspired to learn about what goes on beyond their own church, in other parts of the world and other traditions. Christian magazines, books, websites, radio and TV can all give a new perspective and help bring people to maturity in Christ.

Getting away

Many Christians have benefited from going to conferences, festivals, pilgrimages or Christian holidays (such as Greenbelt, Taizé, Iona, Walsingham, Spring Harvest, New Wine – the list goes on). Many grow through going on a retreat or taking some other structured time away with God (such as a Cursillo weekend). Most dioceses provide guidance in these areas – or try typing 'retreat' into Google, which should take you to the British Retreat Association.

Local and diocesan courses

Most dioceses, and some deaneries, provide courses for deepening learning or discovering and developing skills in ministry. Increasingly, training is organized on a modular basis, and sessions for those preparing for authorized ministries (such as Reader or Ordained Local Ministry) are open for all to participate in, whether they are pursuing a particular ministry or not. This means plenty of opportunity for a ministry candidate to bring a car load of church members with them and learn in depth about particular areas of ministry. Open courses and conferences are also provided by national organizations.

Questions for discussion

1. How many of your church members receive no teaching apart from that given at the main worship event they attend?

2. How much do people learn from the prayers and songs in a service, compared with the formal teaching given?

3. Some teaching starts with a Bible passage, and applies it to life issues; some teaching starts with a life issue and seeks guidance from the Bible. What are the pros and cons of these two approaches?

4. Looking back over the last couple of years, are there any parts of the Bible, or any life issues that have been neglected in the teaching programme?

5. What can be done to encourage greater use of *external* resources for learning and growth?

Walking in the faith: remembering our baptism

One of the chief temptations facing the baptized Christian is to forget their identity in Christ. Evidence for this can be found in the frequent reminders in the New Testament letters urging Christians to recall their status. Paul reminds us that we are 'in Christ', John that we are 'children of God' and Peter that we are 'a chosen race, a royal priesthood, a holy nation, God's own people' (1 Peter 2.9).

'Through baptism a Christian first and finally learns who he or she is. It is the rite of identity.'

William Willimon

> In baptism not only are we commissioned to become who we are in Christ, but we are also given a permanent means of being reminded of that calling. In baptism we discover our spiritual DNA, the pattern of life given to us in Jesus Christ.
>
> In a society that has at best a tenuous grasp of the Christian faith, and where the danger of spiritual amnesia is ever present, how can we help Christians remember their calling?
>
> One of the chief means at our disposal is by keeping the baptismal memory of Christians alive. The purpose of this section is to indicate different ways of recalling our baptism.

Keeping the memory alive

'Hearing and doing these things provides an opportunity to remember our own baptism and reflect on the progress made on that journey, which is now to be shared with this new member of the Church.'

Pastoral Introduction, Holy Baptism, *CWCI*, page 62

Ministers should not underestimate the value of the Baptism service itself in helping every Christian present recall their own baptism. This is one reason why it is important that baptisms be conducted at a main Sunday gathering for worship. As witnesses to others' baptism we learn again of the nature of God's salvation in Christ and we are grateful for the ways in which we have grown deeper into this reality.

There is however specific provision in *Common Worship* which help congregations celebrate and thereby recall the gift of baptism:

Corporate Renewal of Baptismal Vows

Where to find

CW Christian Initiation, pages 193–5
Common Worship: Services and Prayers, pages 149–52

A Form for the Corporate Renewal of Baptismal Vows focuses on the promises made at baptism and is designed to be used within a service other than baptism or confirmation, replacing the Creed. The notes give advice on how and when it is to be used:

> 'This form should be used only when there has been due notice and proper preparation. It is recommended that it is

used no more than once or twice in any one year. Suitable opportunities include Easter, Pentecost, the Baptism of Christ in Epiphany and the inauguration of a new ministry.'

Note 1, page 193

The Renewal of Baptismal Vows draws upon the liturgy of the Baptism service. The congregation is invited to

- respond to the six questions used at the Decision;
- profess faith using the words of the Apostles' Creed;
- use the Affirmation of Commitment from the Commission of adult candidates

Thanksgiving for Holy Baptism

One of the chief limitations of using the title 'Renewal of Baptismal Vows' for a celebration of the gift of baptism is that it only draws attention to one aspect of baptism, our response in faith. If the full memory of baptism is to be celebrated and renewed there needs to be a similar emphasis on God's grace-filled activity signified by and embodied in baptism. This is why the New Zealand bishop Peter Atkins in his book *Memory and Liturgy* argues that the 'Renewal of Baptismal Covenant' would better express both the divine and human dimensions being remembered.

The Thanksgiving for Holy Baptism in *CW Christian Initiation* is a stand-alone service, whereas those in the *Common Worship* main volume and in *Daily Prayer* are for use within Morning or Evening Prayer. Though the first note is slightly specific and prescriptive ('Thanksgiving for Holy Baptism should be made by the newly initiated and the regular congregation some weeks after initiation') the two versions of the service provide a congregation with a valuable means to acknowledge and celebrate *God's grace* in baptism. The minister and people are encouraged to gather around the font for an act of thanksgiving followed by intercession for those recently baptized or preparing for baptism.

One interesting possibility would be to use the Thanksgiving with the Renewal of Baptismal Vows, enabling us to affirm the memory of God's grace alongside our own response of faith. The order of service would be:

- Morning Prayer (which might be the first part of A Service of the Word with Holy Communion) to the Gospel Canticle and Sermon
- Thanksgiving for Holy Baptism (CW, page 48): Introductory responses and thanksgiving prayer

Where to find

Common Worship: Services and Prayers, pages 48–9
Common Worship: Daily Prayer, pages 306–7
CW Christian Initiation, pages 184–7 (an expanded, stand-alone, version of the above)

- The Corporate Renewal of Baptismal Vows (pages 193-5) replaces the Creed (as it always does - see Note 2, page 193)
- Thanksgiving for Holy Baptism (and Morning Prayer) concludes with intercessions, collect and the Peace.

Remembering on the Festival of the Baptism of Christ

The *CW Times and Seasons* volume includes two forms of service for the Festival of the Baptism of Christ. One is a Eucharist and the other a non-eucharistic service. They both include a section for congregational thanksgiving for baptism and re-commitment to their own baptism, drawing on some of the material mentioned above, though neither includes the renewal of baptismal vows.

The use of water

Using water helps members of the congregation make a tangible connection with their own baptism. It has been common in some churches for the corporate Renewal of Baptismal Vows to include water, typically a sprinkling of the congregation by a minister when the renewal is included in Easter Eve celebrations. The rubrics in both the Thanksgiving for Holy Baptism and the Corporate Renewal of Baptismal Vows state that water may be poured into the font and that 'water may be sprinkled over the people or they may be invited to use it to sign themselves with the cross'. This could happen either immediately after the Profession of Faith, or as this part of the service concludes with a hymn or song.

Remembering with children

In the home

The anniversary of a child's baptism gives an opportunity for the family to share in simple rituals that recall the reality of baptism. Here are a few ideas:

- Lighting a candle (the child's baptism candle if possible) as part of a family meal. The lighting could be accompanied by the following words:

In baptism God called *N* out of darkness into his marvellous light.

N, shine as light in the world to the glory of God the Father.

In baptism God calls us all out of darkness into his marvellous light.

Let us shine as lights in the world to the glory of God the Father.

- Gifts could be given (by parents and/or godparents) which have associations with water (bath toys are but one of a number of ideas that imaginative parents might explore!).
- Relive the event by looking at the family photo album or watching the video.

In church

There are a variety of ways in which the church family can foster the remembrance of baptism among children. As with the home, the church is a place to mark anniversaries. For instance, in a monthly parish baptism those children whose anniversaries fall that month could be prayed for publicly (which of course encourages such a service to be held when the children are present).

There could be one or more occasions in the year when children could gather around the font to give thanks for the gift of baptism. This could take place to mark the beginning of the annual cycle of children's groups. The form of Thanksgiving for Holy Baptism (see page 193 above) could be used and one of the various aspects and qualities of water could form the focus. Children could be encouraged to bring their baptism candles (or re-issued ones if the originals have been mislaid or burnt out!). Children who have not been baptized should be welcome there too, as it will help them to begin to realize the importance of baptism.

A prayer of thanksgiving

God in Christ gives us water welling up for eternal life.
With joy you will draw water from the wells of salvation.

Lord, give us this water and we shall thirst no more.

Let us give thanks to the Lord our God.

It is right to give thanks and praise.

Blessed are you, sovereign God of all,
to you be glory and praise for ever.
You are our light and our salvation.

From the deep waters of death
you have raised your Son to life in triumph.
Grant that all who have been born anew by water and the Spirit,
may daily be renewed in your image,
walk by the light of faith,
and serve you in newness of life;
through your anointed Son, Jesus Christ,
to whom with you and the Holy Spirit
we lift our voices of praise.
Blessed be God, Father, Son and Holy Spirit:
Blessed be God for ever.

CWCI, page 184

Remembering day by day

How can we remember our baptism, our status as disciples of Jesus, hour by hour, minute by minute? This is a spiritual challenge beyond the scope of this book, but one to pursue with the help of other authors.

Grant, O Lord, that I may not for one moment
admit willingly into my soul
any thought contrary to thy love.
Amen.

E. B. Pusey 1800–1882

Sharing the faith

E4

The newly baptized are sent out to shine as lights in the world to the glory of God the Father, but the liturgical texts give little explanation of what exactly this means. The candidates are commissioned to serve others *and* to confess the faith of Christ crucified. A key part of Christian discipleship is the call to invite others to walk with us in the way of Christ.

> 'Jesus came and said to them, "All authority in heaven and on earth has been given to me. Go therefore and make disciples of all nations, baptizing them in the name of the Father and of the Son and of the Holy Spirit, and teaching them to obey everything that I have commanded you."'
>
> Matthew 28. 18–20

So what expectations of evangelism might we have of those who are baptized and growing in their faith?

Evangelist? Who, me?

Most people would not think of themselves as evangelists, and only some Christians are specially gifted by God to be evangelists. But all Christians may be involved in the *evangelistic process*. How does this work?

> **'The gifts he gave were that some would be apostles, some prophets, some evangelists, some pastors and teachers, to equip the saints for the work of ministry, for building up the body of Christ.'**
>
> Ephesians 4.11-12

Crisis or process?

There has been a change in our understanding of how people come to faith, and CW *Christian Initiation* recognizes this. There is no longer the expectation that most people who come to faith do so as a result of some kind of a 'Damascus Road' experience, in a single moment of crisis, nudged over the line from 'darkness to light' by an evangelist like Billy Graham. The moment of decision is still there:

'Do you turn to Christ as Saviour?' is one of the questions at the heart of the baptism and confirmation services in a section headed The Decision. But the journey to faith is often quite a long one, and it helps to have some company on the way. Today, fewer and fewer people have any detailed knowledge of the Christian story; they need time to explore and try Christianity on before they commit themselves to it. So there is a collection of resources called Rites Supporting Disciples on the Way of Christ designed to be used with those who commit themselves to this kind of exploration, possibly in a small group.

This shift in understanding from 'crisis' to 'process' has many implications for the evangelistic task, but perhaps the most important is the redefinition of what evangelism actually is. If conversion is just the crisis, the evangelist is someone who helps or persuades people through the moment of decision. But if conversion is more usually a journey, we can redefine *evangelism* as 'anything that helps people move towards God'.

Down the funnel

The theory of Funnel Evangelism is set out clearly in Lawrence Singlehurst's *Sowing, Reaping, Keeping* (IVP, 2006).

Many people have a picture of God as some kind of cruel monster who allows natural disasters to maim and kill children but gets angry at the thought that people might have sex or be gay. In addition, Christians are seen as hypocritical wimps who are only after your money. Therefore our appeals to people to become Christians are actually seen as invitations to believe in a monster and turn into a geek. When you put it like that, you can see why it might not be immediately attractive!

So the first job is to subvert these images by a process called 'GIGAWOK' – a mnemonic for 'God is good and we're OK!' in other words our lifestyle should convince everyone we meet that God is loving and Christians are people to whom they can relate.

Fig. E1

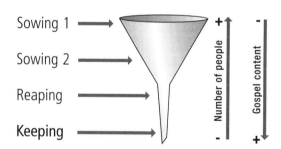

Sowing 1

'Always be ready to make your defence to anyone who demands from you an account of the hope that is in you; yet do it with gentleness and reverence.'

1 Peter 3.15

This is the very top of the funnel, where the number of people involved is greatest but the gospel content is least. Christians are known to be Christians, and they try to cultivate kindness, generosity and care to all with whom they come into contact. You don't have to be a gifted evangelist to be nice to people. Any baptism or confirmation preparation course can stress that this is part of the Christian call to love others: we don't love them simply to move them to conversion, but our loving service may well cause them to ask questions, and that leads us to the next stage ...

Sowing 2

Not all, but some of the people with whom Christians interact will begin to become intrigued and want to know more. They may wistfully admit that 'I wish I could have a faith like yours', particularly during the more difficult times of life. This is where the church comes into play, organizing occasional events that are user-friendly and explain more fully some of the content of the gospel. There is no pressure, simply information.

Events like Christmas carol services, All Souls memorials or more regular guest services can do this well and so can baptism or confirmation services themselves, especially if the candidates will be giving their testimony during the service, and the minister or bishop can be relied upon, if asked, to give an address that will be appropriate for those tentatively exploring faith. The task of the Christians is simply to invite people, but only those who have expressed some interest already.

Reaping

Again, some but not all of those who are beginning to 'try on' the Christian faith will want to go deeper, and may be keen to be part of a group or course specifically aimed at explaining the claims of Christianity and calling for a response. 'Process Evangelism' courses such as Alpha, Emmaus, Saints Alive! and so on serve this purpose. Some people may be helped by having the kind of public enrolment as enquirers which is envisaged, for example, in the Welcome of Disciples on the Way of Faith, with the opportunity to pray for people at this stage in their journey.

[Rites Supporting Disciples on the Way of Christ, *CWCI*, pages 29-56]

And depending on the course being used, the Presentation of the Four Texts (the Summary of the Law, the Lord's Prayer, the Creed and the Beatitudes ➤) may provide useful Bible-based discussion starters for those considering the cost and implications of accepting Christ. The use of the Affirmation of the Christian Way, with its well-rounded view of what is involved in living the Christian life, provides both a possible syllabus and a summary. The last section of this echoes Matthew 28:

➤ **C1**

[*CWCI*, page 36]

> God calls us to share the good news
> *Jesus said, go and make disciples of all nations.*
>
> **Jesus, you are the Way: guide us on our journey.**

If those who come to faith, and to baptism and confirmation, do so through a group like this, some of them may well be the best people

'O taste and see that the Lord is good;
happy are those who take refuge in him.'

Psalm 37.8

to help the next time such a group is run, giving them an opportunity to keep the promise made in the Commission in those services, to 'proclaim by word and example the good news of God in Christ' and to test out their own ability and gift as witnesses and maybe evangelists, challenging people to respond one way or the other to what they have heard and experienced.

Keeping

This is where the witnesses and evangelists hand over to the pastors and teachers who will nurture those who have responded positively to Christ and begin to train them as disciples, teaching them in their turn the principles of evangelism.

Evangelism for all

Will you proclaim by word and example the good news of God in Christ?

With the help of God, I will.

Commission, Holy Baptism, *CWCI*, page 73

We can therefore expect Christians to be a part of the evangelistic process, as long as the church as a whole, and the specially gifted evangelists, are all playing their part in the teamwork. Children may invite their school friends to a church Kidz Klub or Youth Alpha course, even if their theological awareness of all the nuances of the gospel is still a bit sketchy. Adults may become known at work or at the school gates as Christians, and the kind of 'safe people' to whom it is okay to talk about things that really matter without fear of 'getting the Bible rammed down your throat'. They certainly should be known as the kindest, most caring and considerate people around, rather than the weirdest! Families might work together using hospitality or practical acts of kindness to reach out to other families with the love of Christ. But it is important then that the church and its evangelists are backing up the process for those who want to go deeper.

'The journey continues ... as the community continues to work out together the meaning of Christian belonging and the imperative to share the good news of the kingdom of God with others.'

Commentary, *CWCI*, page 326

Questions for discussion

1. Is there enough in your preparation of candidates for baptism or confirmation that equips and enthuses them for the task of sharing the faith that they will be proclaiming at the service?

2. Are you using the opportunities of baptism and confirmation services as opportunities to invite guests?

3. Have you considered the Rites Supporting Disciples on the Way of Christ and how they could strengthen the link between worship and evangelism in your church?

E5 Return and reconciliation

Coming back

Jesus told a parable of the son who took his inheritance, went away, and squandered it on wine, women, and song. When the money ran out he was destitute, his new friends deserted him, and he ended up feeding pigs – a particularly distasteful thing for a Jewish lad to have to do. When virtually starving, he remembered his father and resolved to confess his folly and return home. He was met with open arms of welcome. The story of the 'prodigal son' is a well-loved gospel story that reflects the life of many people. It is a story of returning to faith. The new rites of Reconciliation and Restoration include a number of services that may help people in their journey back to faith.

[Luke 15.11-32]

Deborah was baptized a child in a churchgoing family. She was involved in various church activities as she grew up, getting confirmed at the same time as others in the youth group. She went to university but could not get on with the Christian groups. She drifted from church, made new friends and started going clubbing. She had a number of short, stormy relationships, and then lived with someone for a number of years.

As time progressed, her career developed and she wanted to have children. She married her partner, and their first child was soon born. Though her husband had no faith, they had been married in church and she now wanted her daughter baptized. Birth had been a profound experience and her thoughts were returning to the God she remembered as a child. She was also painfully aware of some of the things she had done in the past, and particular words said to different people at the end of some relationships. Her renewed experience of the love of Christ prompted her to ask the vicar about those things that she had done that weighed heavily in her heart and which she could not seem to deal with by herself. She asked about 'confession' hoping that this might help her.

Some people are baptized and confirmed and then stray from the faith. Nevertheless, God's Spirit continues to speak in their hearts, calling them back to the Way, and giving them a thirst for worship and fellowship. Any church that declares the good news of God's love and forgiveness should be openly encouraging those who – however tentatively – venture to return, and should be prepared and willing to welcome them back. Some will want to come quietly with the minimum of fuss, but others may wish to make a fresh commitment. This can be a public service such as the Affirmation of Baptismal Faith. ☛ For many this will be sufficient. But some are troubled by memories of actions that have deeply hurt themselves and others, and were seriously wrong. Pastoral counselling will help some of these, and might for them be sufficient. For other people the rites of reconciliation and restoration may be a useful provision as a part of their return to faith.

Individual and corporate

The rites of reconciliation and restoration include both corporate and individual rites. The individual rite has a number of key elements in it:

- careful preparation
- explanation of the process
- readings of scripture, including from Psalm 51
- confession and counsel
- act (prayer) of contrition
- absolution
- thanksgiving
- blessing

For some people this more 'formal' procedure is for them a helpful way of dealing with their sinful actions. For many this will be a one-off event that helps them to return to Christian life and enables them to put the past behind them. The process may entail them writing letters of apology, or taking practical steps to put right what they can.

Helping an individual

All Christians sin, but the sins of some become public. The Church has a number of ways to minister the gospel of reconciliation. Confession is a regular part of Anglican worship but in some cases is insufficient to deal with the situation. People's sins are discovered producing public scandal in areas such as theft, fraud, illegal action, sexual misconduct, and public acrimony. Churches need to be able to restore the fallen to fellowship, and the services for the Reconciliation of a Penitent in *CW Christian Initiation* are designed for this situation. It is devastating to be caught, abandoned by the Church, and then feel there is no way of return. Reconciliation and restoration is costly on both sides. The Church still has much to learn from stepped programmes, such as Alcoholics Anonymous,

☛D12

'The resources and forms of service for Reconciliation and Restoration are intended to meet some of the situations in which the Church confronts the fact of human weakness and sin and appropriates again the new life proclaimed in baptism.'

Commentary, *CWCI*, page 353

[*CWCI*, page 267]

'Healing, reconciliation and restoration are integral to the good news of Jesus Christ. For this reason prayer for individuals … has a proper place within the public prayer of the Church.'

Commentary, *CWCI*, page 354

Tom was the church treasurer. The church was quite well off and so he had large amounts of money to manage. He was increasingly getting into debt as he tried to keep his family in the lifestyle they had grown to expect. One year his bonuses were cut and he could not keep up debt payments. He began to 'borrow' from the church without telling anyone. Soon he was dependent on this borrowing to stay afloat. As his debts got bigger so he borrowed more. Eventually, in spite of carefully covering his tracks, he was caught and taken to court. He received a short prison sentence. He felt awful, moved house, but still wanted to go to church, but what he had done had been in the papers. He decided to ask for confession and forgiveness to start again.

about restoring the lost. 'The receiving of forgiveness and the act of forgiving others may open the way to healing and wholeness' (page 354).

Expressing penitence together

In some circumstances division arises in the Christian fellowship. This needs a *different* approach from the more individual confession.

A Corporate Service of Penitence is intended for use, if desired, as part of the seasonal worship of the Church (for instance, in Lent or Advent), or as an expression of a desire for renewal. Surprisingly, it is *not* intended for use in response to an event or situation, such as the one described alongside, and if it is adapted for this purpose (which in some circumstances may be more helpful than starting with a blank sheet) the Bishop's direction should be followed (page 228, note 1).

However, the service may be used for the restoration of individuals in a corporate setting. This might be appropriate when an individual has harmed the whole fellowship.

Service outline

The service may include Holy Communion, in which case the outline can be as described here.

The Gathering
The Greeting, introduction and comfortable words

Collect

The Liturgy of the Word
Readings

Sermon

Prayer and Penitence
The Liturgy of the Sacrament
The Sending Out

Either Thanksgiving for Holy Baptism
or Proclamation of the Gospel

Dismissal

The choir at St Mary's had a long tradition, but few new members. A new vicar came and wanted to introduce new hymns. This was well received by many but a few, including many of the choir, were resistant. A music group began for the flourishing family service, but the choir continued in the traditional way at other services. Tension grew between the groups. At one AGM the organist exploded and resigned. Half the choir threatened to leave, boycotting the services. This made a headline in the local paper. Careful pastoral work by the churchwardens and vicar led to new understandings and all began to see a place for themselves in the life of St Mary's. A special service of reconciliation was planned and was a highlight of the year. Tears were shed by some in the sharing of the Peace.

[A Corporate Service of Penitence (*CWCI*, pages 228-63) builds on the Penitential Services previously published in *Lent, Holy Week, Easter* and *Promise of His Glory*]

This section of the book includes a large amount of resource material (pages 240-63), which can be flexibly related to the pastoral context.

> Teach us, who live only in your forgiveness,
> to forgive one another; heal our divisions and cast out our fears.
>
> Page 240

Questions for discussion

1. How easy would you find it to come back to your church, if you had not been involved for some time because you felt you had let yourself and God down?

2. How would you start? What would make it easier for you?

3. How could your church make it easier for somebody to know God's forgiveness and come back?

The Sending Out

In *The Book of Common Prayer*, Baptism is an 'occasional office', suitable for incorporating the newly born into the established Church of a society which was presumed to be largely Christianized. The only hint of any mission implications is the opinion in the Preface (which underlines what a different world the *BCP* was written for) that the new adult baptism service 'may be useful for baptizing the natives in our plantations, and others converted to the faith'. Times have changed, and so have our ideas about the nature of the Church and our relationship to our society, and therefore about baptism. Baptism is no longer an occasional office.

CW Christian Initiation is a tool for mission which both emerges out of, and continues to contribute to, our new understanding of the centrality of baptism to the mission of the Church. We have seen throughout this book ways in which these resources can be used as an integral part of that mission. Many things contribute to the mission impact of the various parts of Christian Initiation – and might suitably be part of the agenda for a periodic review of the local church's initiation programme:

- The welcome given to enquirers and visitors by the whole congregation.
- The way in which the services are taken.
- The presentation of materials, texts, service sheets and invitations.
- The involvement of candidates and others in the catechumenal process.
- The production development and implementation of a mission-centred local policy for baptism and confirmation.
- The awareness on the part of the members of the local church of the issues involved.
- The use of individual services such as the Thanksgiving for the Gift of a Child, Affirmation and Reception, and the provisions to encourage people returning to the faith.
- The way in which the whole process is enveloped in prayer.

The hope of the contributors and editors of this book is that it will not only deepen the understanding of local church members but stimulate the kind of action which sees all of the resources of *CW Christian Initiation* being used in the mission and growth of the Church.

> 'Go ... and make disciples of all nations, baptizing them in the name of the Father and of the Son and of the Holy Spirit, and teaching them to obey everything that I have commanded you.'
>
> Matthew 28.19–20

Appendix: Canon Law

The relevant parts of Section B of The Church of England's Canon Law, on Divine Service and the administration of the sacraments are provided here for ease of reference, and so that the excerpts from it scattered throughout the book can be seen in context. The Introduction to *CW Christian Initiation* (page 5) gives a hint of an approach to the legal standing of the texts themselves: 'The authorized texts and the commended liturgical provision need to be seen not primarily as legal regulation but rather as a guide to a coherent celebration of the rite.'

The authorization page (page 1) summarizes **Canon B3**:

> 'Canon B 3 provides that decisions as to which of the authorized services are to be used (other than occasional offices) shall be taken jointly by the incumbent and the parochial church council. In the case of occasional offices (other than Confirmation and Ordination), the decision is to be made by the minister conducting the service, subject to the right of any of the persons concerned to object beforehand to the form of service proposed.'

B 21 Of Holy Baptism

It is desirable that every minister having a cure of souls shall normally administer the sacrament of Holy Baptism on Sundays at public worship when the most number of people come together, that the congregation there present may witness the receiving of them that be newly baptized into Christ's Church, and be put in remembrance of their own profession made to God in their baptism.

B 22 Of the baptism of infants

1. Due notice, normally of at least a week, shall be given before a child is brought to the church to be baptized.

2. If the minister shall refuse or unduly delay to baptize any such infant, the parents or guardians may apply to the bishop of the diocese, who shall, after consultation with the minister, give such directions as he thinks fit.

3. The minister shall instruct the parents or guardians of an infant to be admitted to Holy Baptism that the same responsibilities rest on them as are in the service of Holy Baptism required of the godparents.

4. No minister shall refuse or, save for the purpose of preparing or instructing the parents or guardians or godparents, delay to baptize any infant within his cure that is brought to the church to be baptized, provided that due notice has been given and the provisions relating to godparents in these Canons are observed.

5. A minister who intends to baptize any infant whose parents are residing outside the boundaries of his cure, unless the names of such persons or of one of them be on the church electoral roll of the same, shall not proceed to the baptism without having sought the good will of the minister of the parish in which such parents reside.

6. No minister being informed of the weakness or danger of death of any infant within his cure and therefore desired to go to baptize the same shall either refuse or delay to do so.

7. A minister so baptizing a child in a hospital or nursing home, the parents of the child not being resident in his cure, nor their names on the church electoral roll of the same, shall send their names and address to the minister of the parish in which they reside.

8. If any infant which is privately baptized do afterwards live, it shall be brought to the church and there, by the minister, received into the congregation of Christ's flock according to the form and manner prescribed in and by the office for Private Baptism authorized by Canon B 1.

9. The minister of every parish shall warn the people that without grave cause and necessity they should not have their children baptized privately in their houses.

B 23 Of godparents and sponsors

1. For every child to be baptized there shall be not fewer than three godparents, of whom at least two shall be of the same sex as the child and of whom at least one shall be of the opposite sex; save that, when three cannot conveniently be had, one godfather and godmother shall suffice. Parents may be godparents for their own children provided that the children have at least one other godparent.

2. The godparents shall be persons who will faithfully fulfil their responsibilities both by their care for the children committed to their charge and by the example of their own godly living.

3. When one who is of riper years is to be baptized he shall choose three, or at least two, to be his sponsors, who shall be ready to present him at the font and afterwards put him in mind of his Christian profession and duties.

4. No person shall be admitted to be a sponsor or godparent who has not been baptized and confirmed. Nevertheless the minister shall have power to dispense with the requirement of confirmation in any case in which in his judgement need so requires.

B 24 Of the baptism of such as are of riper years

1. When any such person as is of riper years and able to answer for himself is to be baptized, the minister shall instruct such person, or cause him to be instructed, in the principles of the Christian religion, and exhort him so to prepare himself with prayers and fasting that he may receive this holy sacrament with repentance and faith.

2. At least a week before any such baptism is to take place, the minister shall give notice thereof to the bishop of the diocese or whomsoever he shall appoint for the purpose.

3. Every person thus baptized shall be confirmed by the bishop so soon after his baptism as conveniently may be; that so he may be admitted to the Holy Communion.

B 25 Of the sign of the Cross in baptism

The Church of England has ever held and taught, and holds and teaches still, that the sign of the Cross used in baptism is no part of the substance of the sacrament: but, for the remembrance of the Cross, which is very precious to those that rightly believe in Jesus Christ, has retained the sign of it in baptism, following therein the primitive and apostolic Churches.

B 26 Of teaching the young

1. Every minister shall take care that the children and young people within his cure are instructed in the doctrine, sacraments, and discipline of Christ, as the Lord has commanded and as they are set forth in the Holy Scriptures, in *The Book of Common Prayer*, and especially in the Church Catechism; and to this end he, or some godly and competent persons appointed by him, shall on Sundays or if need be at other convenient times diligently instruct and teach them in the same.

2. All parents and guardians shall take care that their children receive such instruction.

B 27 Of confirmation

1. The bishop of every diocese shall himself minister (or cause to be ministered by some other bishop lawfully deputed in his stead) the rite of confirmation throughout his diocese as often and in as many places as shall be convenient, laying his hands upon children and other persons who have been baptized and instructed in the Christian faith.

2. Every minister who has a cure of souls shall diligently seek out children and other persons whom he shall think meet to be confirmed and shall use his best endeavour to instruct them in the Christian faith and life as set forth in the Holy Scriptures, *The Book of Common Prayer*, and the Church Catechism.

3. The minister shall present none to the bishop but such as are come to years of discretion and can say the Creed, the Lord's Prayer, and the Ten Commandments, and can also render an account of their faith according to the said Catechism.

4. The minister shall satisfy himself that those whom he is to present have been validly baptized, ascertaining the date and place of such baptism, and, before or at the time assigned for the confirmation, shall give to the bishop their names, together with their age and the date of their baptism.

5. If the minister is doubtful about the baptism of a candidate for confirmation he shall conditionally baptize him in accordance with the form of service authorized by Canon B 1 before presenting him to the bishop to be confirmed.

6. If it is desired for sufficient reason that a Christian name be changed, the bishop may, under the laws of this realm, confirm a person by a new Christian name, which shall be thereafter deemed the lawful Christian name of such person.

B 28 Of reception into the Church of England

1. Any person desiring to be received into the Church of England, who has not been baptized or the validity of whose baptism can be held in question, shall be instructed and baptized or conditionally baptized, and such baptism, or conditional baptism, shall constitute the said person's reception into the Church of England.

2. If any such person has been baptized but not episcopally confirmed and desires to be formally admitted into the Church of England he shall, after appropriate instruction, be received by the rite of confirmation, or, if he be not yet ready to be presented

for confirmation, he shall be received by the parish priest with appropriate prayers.

3. If any such person has been episcopally confirmed with unction or with the laying on of hands he shall be instructed, and, with the permission of the bishop, received into the Church of England according to the Form of Reception approved by the General Synod, or with other appropriate prayers, and if any such person be a priest he shall be received into the said Church only by the bishop of the diocese or by the commissary of such bishop.

Index

Note: Page references in **bold** type indicate material in text margins; those in *italics* indicate diagrams. The abbreviation CofE is used for Church of England.

Index of biblical references